GOLDEN AGE

Commercial Aviation in Britain 1945–1965

BEA's inaugural jet service from Manchester. Trident 1 G-ARPO waits to depart for Paris (Le Bourget) on 1 July 1965. In the background is the new control tower and a BEA Vanguard.

GOLDEN AGE

Commercial Aviation in Britain
1945–1965

Charles Woodley

Airlife

England

Copyright © 1992 by Charles Woodley

First published in the UK in 1992
by Airlife Publishing Ltd.

British Library Cataloguing in Publication Data
A catalogue record for this book
is available from the British Library

ISBN 1 85310 259 8

Printed by Livesey Ltd., Shrewsbury

Airlife Publishing Ltd.
101 Longden Road, Shrewsbury SY3 9EB

Contents

	Introduction and Acknowledgements	7
Chapter 1	Prelude to the Fifties	9
Chapter 2	Farewell to the Flying Boats	17
Chapter 3	The Decline of Northolt and Croydon	21
Chapter 4	The Growth of Heathrow	27
Chapter 5	The Trans-Atlantic Struggle	43
Chapter 6	The Rebirth of Gatwick	55
Chapter 7	Regional Scheduled Services	61
Chapter 8	Colonial Coach Services	95
Chapter 9	Trooping Flights	99
Chapter 10	Coach-Air and Rail-Air	105
Chapter 11	Car Ferries	109
Chapter 12	Ad Hoc Charter Flights	113
Chapter 13	Inclusive Tour Charters	119
Chapter 14	General Aviation	129
Chapter 15	The Way Things Might Have Been	143
	Bibliography	149
	Major Airliner Types 1950–1965	151
	Index	157

British Eagle V.739 Viscount G-ATDR *City of Truro* transits Manchester on 29 August 1965 with flight EG690/691 from Liverpool to Ostend.

Introduction and Acknowledgements

I became an aviation enthusiast at the end of the 1950s, after spending most of my childhood indulging in that other schoolboy passion — train spotting. The disappearance of steam from the railways and a growing awareness of the constant stream of propeller-driven airliners passing overhead on their way into nearby London Airport perhaps made it inevitable that I should turn my attention to the skies and that my new-found interest should focus on commercial aviation rather than military.

Looking back now from the high-tech, security-conscious 1990s it seems as if I entered a different world on my first visits to the spectators' enclosures at London Airport and Gatwick, a world of graceful piston-engined airliners and small airlines struggling to make a living with a handful of semi-obsolete aircraft. Many of these companies failed to survive for more than a year or two but others prospered and went on to become major influences in the air transport industry.

The story of their struggle is contained within these pages, from the dark days immediately after the Berlin Airlift when many operators found themselves without work for their fleets, to the introduction of trans-Atlantic jet airliners in the 1960s. It is a story that encompasses the whole of the United Kingdom and features some airfields that were major commercial airports in their time but have since been relegated to less prestigious flying activities or to just fond memories. I have found this story fascinating and I hope that you too will find something of historical and nostalgic interest in this account of a 'Golden Age' of aviation in Britain.

Such a story could not have been written without much generous help and encouragement from very many organisations and individuals. I would particularly like to thank: Alan Scholefield, Peter Pallett, Barry Abraham, Capt. John Morris (for the loan of photographs from the Air Britain archives), my old pals from BKS Barry Williams and David Jones, Brian Robinson of Manchester Airport Archives, Mr D.R. Ellis of Luton International Airport, Mrs B. McFarlane, Mrs N. Ogden, Mr D. Sutcliffe, Mr A.H. Spettigue, Peter Batten of Westland Helicopters, Malcolm D. Stride, Frank D. Price, Jonathan Easthope, E.T.W. Dennis & Sons, Steve Bond, Michael Wall, Mr F. Smallwood, Peter Maddocks, Mrs H. Fidgeon (for kindly donating the Croydon photos of the late Mr L.A. Holmes), the Public Relations staffs of QANTAS, SABENA, Lufthansa, Pan American World Airways, the writers and publishers of *British Independent Airlines since 1946* (for producing such an excellent source of reference) and finally my wife Hazel and our children for supporting me in my first venture into authorship and for putting up with my reclusive behaviour during the gestation period of this book.

This book is not intended as a historical or technical textbook and so I have taken some liberties with generalisations in the interests of simplicity of narrative. For instance, all DC-3 and C-47 variants are referred to throughout as Dakotas and all C-54s in airline service appear as DC-4s. Similarly, where two or more reputable sources disagree over the exact date of an event I have quoted the version favoured by the majority.

Photo Credits

The author and publishers are grateful to the following for permission to reproduce copyright photographs: Aberdeen Journals Ltd, 66; Barry H. Abraham, 74, 85, 94, 100, 121, 131, 134 (bottom), 135, 136, 137, 138; Air Britain Archives, 16 (top), 19, 20 (top), 53, 54, 57, 59 (top), 67, 70, 73, 84, 106, 115, 118, 126, 127, 133, 134 (top), 141 (bottom), 142, 145; BEA, 22, 25 (top), 29, 87; BOAC, 26, 42, 44; British Aerospace, 30, 37, 51, 96; *Cheshire Life,* 78; E.T.W. Dennis & Sons, 76; Norman Edwards Associates (Manchester) Ltd, 15; Mr D. R. Ellis, Luton International Airport, 98, 114, 122, 124; the late Mr L. A. Holmes, 20 (bottom), 92; David Jones, 34; Peter Maddocks, 132; Mrs B. P. McFarlane, 60; Manchester Airport Archives, *frontispiece,* 78, 80; Mrs N. Ogden, 75; Peter Pallett, 103; Pan-American World Airways, 10, 45; Frank D. Price via Jonathan Easthope, 16 (bottom), 40, 88, 89, 125, 128; QANTAS, 38; SABENA Belgian World Airways, 32, 46, 81, 111; R. A. Scholefield, 6, 101, 108, 140; Mr F. Smallwood, 71; Mr A. H. Spettigue, 41; Malcolm D. Stride, 36, 47; Westland Helicopters, 13, 35, 147.

Chapter 1

Prelude to the Fifties

On the resumption of civil aviation in Britain after World War Two there was little that could justifiably be called 'commercial aviation' in the strictest sense as most of the air services of the time were hopelessly uneconomical. The long distance schedules of the British Overseas Airways Corporation (BOAC) were operated either by flying-boats, which were comfortable and popular with passengers but had very limited applications, or by war-surplus transports or converted bombers which were unable to carry a profitable payload on most routes. European services were flown initially by the RAF pending the establishment of British European Airways (BEA) and the domestic air routes were still under the overall control of the Associated Airways Joint Committee, which had been set up in May 1940 to co-ordinate internal air travel under wartime restrictions. Aer Lingus flights from neutral Eire to the UK had however continued to operate with relatively few interruptions throughout the war years.

In 1943 the decision had been taken to build near to London an RAF bomber aerodrome capable of handling the heaviest warplanes then envisaged. With eventual victory in mind consideration was also given to conversion of the airfield for airline use in due course. Construction work on the site at Heathrow near Hounslow began in 1944 and the main east/west runway was ready for use by September 1945.

1945 saw BOAC operating a motley fleet of 169 aircraft of nineteen different types and fitted with nineteen types of engine. Typical of the stop-gap aircraft pressed into commercial service in the immediate post-war years was the Avro Lancastrian, which was used by BOAC and QANTAS of Australia from 1945 on their schedules to Sydney. The aircraft was a crude conversion of the Lancaster bomber, with nose and tail cones in place of the gun turrets. It cruised at 230 mph and had a maximum range of 4150 miles. The journey to Australia took sixty hours and only nine passengers could be carried on each flight. Not surprisingly the service sustained losses of £1.4 million each year. The same aircraft type was also used by the British South American Airways Corporation (BSAAC) to inaugurate their route to Buenos Aires, Santiago and Lima in 1946, carrying 13 passengers on each trip.

On 1 January 1946 the new airport at Heathrow was formerly handed over to the Ministry of Civil Aviation by the Air Ministry. It was officially named London Airport by Lord Winster, the Minister of Aviation, in a ceremony on 25 March 1946.

On 16 April Panair Do Brasil L-049 Constellation PP-PCF landed on a proving flight from Rio to become the first Constellation and the first aircraft of a foreign airline to land at London Airport. The first BOAC scheduled flight to use the airport was the joint 'Kangaroo' service with QANTAS which departed for Australia on 28 May. Prior to this BOAC had been using Hurn Airport at Bournemouth as their London landplane terminus. The last BOAC scheduled service from Hurn was an Avro York flight to Cairo on 14 June but the airline continued to use Hurn for crew training and as a bad weather alternative for some years.

The Yorks were also allocated to BOAC's Johannesburg services. Thirteen of them were fitted out as twelve-berth sleepers and the other eighteen in the fleet were equipped with eighteen seats for daytime use. Twelve of the type were also used by BSAAC on their routes to South America.

Pan American Airways L-0 Constellation NC 88860 *Clipper Lond* rests at London Airport on 1 June 19 after operating the airline's first N York-London service into the ne airport. London Airport had be officially opened on the previous day a the primitive passenger facilities of t time can be seen in the background.

Another airline flying initially into Hurn was American Overseas Airlines, which was the first airline to operate a scheduled landplane passenger service across the North Atlantic. On 23-24 October 1945 they unaugurated a DC-4 schedule from New York which was upgraded to L-049 Constellation equipment in 1946.

London Airport was officially opened on 31 May 1946 and on that date the first trans-Atlantic scheduled flights arrived in the shape of Constellations of Pan American Airways and American Overseas Airlines. BOAC introduced their own Constellations on 1 July 1946 after a proving flight from New York to London on 16 June. Two round trips were made each week at first but this frequency was soon increased to daily. The Constellations reduced the westbound journey time to under 20 hours but stops were still necessary at Shannon or Prestwick and at Gander. Services to Canada were provided by Trans-Canada Air Lines. In 1946 they provided five flights each week from London and Prestwick to Montreal with Avro Lancastrians. The single fare from London to Montreal was £85 at this time.

On 1 January 1946 the British European Airways Division of BOAC was formally constituted and from 4 February it took over the Continental routes formerly operated by No. 110 Wing of RAF Transport Command. Initially however the Dakota fleet continued to carry RAF markings and the crews still wore RAF uniforms. Operations were transferred from Croydon to RAF Northolt near Uxbridge with the exception of the Rapide services to the Channel Islands which did not relocate until 1 November 1947. On 1 March 1946 Northolt officially became a civil airport on loan from the RAF to the Ministry of Civil Aviation.

The British European Airways Corporation was established on 31 August 1946 under the Civil Aviation Act of 1946. From that date BEA operated services to the Continent in their own right but the domestic routes continued to be flown on BEA's behalf by the independent airlines under the supervision of the AAJC. BEA's initial fleet consisted of twenty-one Dakotas but on 1 September 1946 these were supplemented by the first of the Corporation's Vickers Vikings, which entered service that day on a four-times weekly schedule to Copenhagen. BEA established their main engineering base at Northolt and set up their head office in Bourne School (later renamed Keyline House) on the eastern side of the airport.

At this time Aer Lingus held a monopoly on scheduled services between Eire and the United Kingdom, under the terms of an agreement in which BEA took a thirty per cent (later increased to forty per cent) shareholding in the Irish national airline.

Another London area airfield became available for commercial use in August 1946 when RAF Gatwick was de-commissioned and the decision was taken to operate it as a charter airport for a trial period of six months. The Ministry of Civil Aviation provided the necessary facilities and in November Gatwick became a customs airport once more. Among the first residents were the MCA themselves, using a fleet of Avro 19s, Airspeed Consuls, Austers

and Percival Proctors for examining candidates for the Commercial Pilot's Licence and for calibrating airfield landing aids.

BEA finally took over the domestic air routes from the AAJC airlines in February 1947. The BEA fleet at 31 March 1947 comprised twenty-two Dakotas, eleven 'Jupiter' class JU52/3Ms, twenty-nine Vikings, forty-five Rapides and twelve Avro 19s. The Vikings were introduced on to the internal network on 11 August with a Northolt-Glasgow (Renfrew) service. BOAC's fleet in 1947 totalled 147 aircraft but these were of many different types, most of which were uneconomical to operate, and even if 100 per cent load factors had been achieved the airline was not in a position to break even until after 1950.

One aircraft that was able to make money for its operators was the Lockheed Constellation which QANTAS placed onto the 'Kangaroo' service from Australia in place of Lancastrians in December 1947. The first Constellation flight carried thirty-eight First Class passengers and ten crew and made the journey to London in 55 hours 7 minutes.

BEA Sikorsky S-51 G-AKCU lands at Mudford near Yeovil during dummy scheduled helicopter mail services carried out in the West Country during early 1948.

By the end of 1947 an additional runway had been completed at London Airport and two more were almost ready. During that summer over 130,000 passengers passed through the airport.

From May 1948 the private airlines were once again permitted to operate domestic scheduled flights under BEA Associate Agreements, but these were usually restricted to routes which BEA had no interest in operating themselves.

The first such Agreement was awarded to Western Airways in conjunction with Cambrian Air Services for a route from Weston-Super-Mare to Cardiff (Pengam Moors) Airport. Avro Ansons were used and the first service was flown on 25 May 1948.

On 27 January 1948 BEA began operating dummy mail services by helicopter over a scheduled 115-mile routing which began and finished at Yeovil. S-51 helicopters were used and including ten en-route stops the journey took 1 hour 55 minutes. The operation continued until 7 March, with only twenty-three of the 570 scheduled calls being cancelled because of adverse weather or technical problems, and timekeeping was within the five minute margin acceptable to the GPO. BEA then began carrying real letters by helicopter from 1 June 1948, again using S-51s, on what was the first helicopter-operated public mail service in the UK. A dozen points in East Anglia were served on a circular route from Peterborough. The flights continued until 25 September and 98.4 per cent of the scheduled calls were carried out.

In July 1948 the Soviet authorities closed the road, rail and waterway access points between Berlin and Western Europe, effectively isolating the city. The decision was taken to supply the city with the essentials of life by air, and on 27 July 1948 the Berlin Airlift began. Initially the airlift was maintained by the RAF and USAAF but it was soon realised that they could not cope with the demand alone and the British charter operators were invited to participate under overall military control. The first flight of the Civil

Airlift took place on 4 August 1948 when an Avro Lancastrian tanker of Flight Refuelling Ltd. carried a load of fuel direct to Berlin from its base at Tarrant Rushton.

The most widely used aircraft on the Civil Airlift were the ubiquitous Dakotas and converted Halifax bombers. The Treasury was offering £85 per flying hour to Halifax operators and among those who took up this offer was Mr Harold Bamberg, who had founded his Eagle Aviation company with a single Halifax. He paid £500 for the aircraft and spent a further £3500 on the construction of a special freight pannier which fitted under the bomb bay. Among the more unusual aircraft taking part in the Airlift were two Short Sunderland flying-boats which were used by Aquila Airways to carry meat, flour and salt from Finkenwerder on the River Elbe to Lake Havel in Berlin until the threat of winter ice on the lake forced their withdrawal. By the time the Airlift ended on 16 August 1949 the civil operators had completed 21,785 flights into Berlin.

The Airlift had provided a financial breathing space for the struggling charter airlines during 1948 and 1949 but after it ended there was no work for dozens of these companies. Many had to cease operations but among the survivors were some which were to prosper and make a major contribution in the next decade including Silver City Airways, Eagle Aviation, Skyways and Airwork Ltd.

One company that made money by staying out of the Berlin Airlift was Aviation Traders Ltd., which had been founded after the war by Mr Freddie Laker. He had attended a war surplus sale and bought ninety-nine Halifax bombers at £100 each plus spare engines at £5 a piece. These were not operated by Aviation Traders but were instead broken up for scrap metal. Shortly before the beginning of the Airlift Freddie Laker also purchased a fleet of twelve Halton conversions of the Halifax bomber and a large stock of spares from BOAC. Six aircraft were resold and the others were leased to Bond Air Services for use on the Airlift. From their massive stockpile of Halifax parts Aviation Traders sold replacement engines and spares to all of the major users of the type. After the Airlift was over their engineers at Southend Airport constructed a brick-lined tank with a gas burner at the bottom. Into this over the next year went the dismantled remains of hundreds of redundant Halifaxes and other aircraft, whose reduction to scrap metal kept the company in business during the post-Airlift recession.

Another unexpected opportunity for the charter airlines to earn some welcome revenue came at the end of August 1948 when an acute milk shortage in mainland Britain resulted in a milk airlift from Northern Ireland. During the period to the end of October 50,000 gallons were flown across the Irish Sea from Nutts Corner in Belfast to Squires Gate Airport, Blackpool and Speke Airport, Liverpool. A combined fleet of two Liberator bomber conversions, six Halifaxes, and five Dakotas belonging to seven different airlines including Scottish Airlines and the Lancashire Aircraft Corporation flew the milk across in ten-gallon churns, seventy in each Halifax and fifty-six per Dakota.

In an attempt to stimulate still further the growing public interest in air transport the *Daily Express* sponsored an Air Pageant at Gatwick Airport in 1948. Some 70,000 spectators were treated to a display which included a fly-past of the latest airliners including a DC-6 of KLM and a BSAAC Tudor 4. This successful venture was repeated at Gatwick in 1949.

An early step along the road that would eventually lead to the Autoland systems of today was taken on 30 November 1948 when an Airwork Viking took off from Blackbushe Airport, near Camberley, with a cargo of urgently needed currency for West Africa by using the FIDO fog-dispersal system. This was the first time that FIDO had been used on a commercial service.

On 30 July 1949 BSAAC was merged into BOAC under the terms of the 1949 Airways Corporations Act. During the year BOAC took delivery of their new Canadair Argonaut fleet. The final aircraft was delivered on 11 November, marking the fulfilment of the order a full eight months ahead of the contract date.

The inaugural Aer Lingus Dublin-Birmingham service during turnround at Elmdon Airport on 2 May 1949. The airport buildings still bear the signs of wartime service. Note the shamrock flag flying from the cockpit roof of C-47A Dakota EI-ACL *St Declan*.

The most significant aviation event that year though took place on 27 July when the prototype De Havilland Comet jet airliner made its maiden flight, pointing the way to the future of commercial aviation, not only in Britain but throughout the world.

BOAC Solent G-AHIO *Somerset* clearly showing the window layout of the twin-deck cabin.

A BOAC Short Solent in a suitably maritime setting, circa 1950.

Chapter 2

Farewell to the Flying Boats

BOAC used a large fleet of flying boats to re-open routes to Africa, the Far East and Australia from 1946 onwards, initially using Poole in Dorset as their UK terminus. The flying boats were restricted to operations from suitable marine bases however and many new airfields with long runways had been constructed during World War Two. These had the potential to accept the new and large landplane airliners being offered to the airlines and so the operationally inflexible flying boats were gradually superceded until their final retirement from BOAC service in 1950.

The mixed BOAC fleet included 24 'Hythe' class conversions of the Short Sunderland patrol aircraft. These were configured to carry twenty-two day time or sixteen night passengers on routes to Singapore, Hong Kong and Australia. When they were replaced by Lockheed Constellations in 1949 the 'Hythes' had flown twenty-five million miles in BOAC service and carried 79,793 passengers.

BOAC also used twelve Short Solent conversions of the military Seaford design. These were delivered between 1946 and April 1948 and the final example G-AHIY was the last aircraft ever built at the Short Bros. seaplane works at Rochester. The Solent carried seven crew and up to thirty passengers on two decks. The lower deck contained three cabin compartments, promenade, library and wardrobe compartments, dressing rooms and toilets. The entire aircraft was air-conditioned and a spiral staircase provided access to the upper deck which featured a cocktail bar, cabin-lounge, steward's compartment and a fully equipped galley containing refrigerators and electric cookers.

The new BOAC flying-boat terminal at Berth 50 Southampton Water was officially opened on 14 April 1948, although the first service to use the facility had arrived there on 31 March and the first departure was on 1 April to Sydney. The Solent fleet entered service on 4 May 1948 with a flight to Johannesburg (Vaaldam). The journey was scheduled to take four and a half days with three nightstops en route.

On 5 May 1949 BOAC Solent 3 G-AKNO landed on the River Thames and taxied to the Tower of London where it was moored as part of the celebrations to mark the thirtieth anniversary of British civil aviation.

BOAC replaced their Solent flying-boat service from Southampton to Lake Naiwasha near Nairobi with a Handley Page Hermes 4 landplane operation from 24 September 1950 and on 7 November the Solent schedule to Johannesburg was also taken over by Hermes aircraft. The Solents were then withdrawn, thus terminating the last BOAC flying-boat service and ending an association with flying-boats that BOAC and its predecessor Imperial Airways had maintained since 1924.

This was not the end of the line for all of BOAC's machines however as many of them were purchased by Aquila Airways. Aquila Airways was registered as a company in May 1948 and took part in the Berlin Airlift, flying two Short Sunderland flying-boats from Finkenwerder on the River Elbe to Lake Havel in Berlin.

On 24–25 March 1949 the airline made the first survey flight over their proposed route from Southampton to Lisbon and Funchal in Madeira with a 'Hythe' class Sunderland. Regular services began on 11 June 1949 on a fortnightly 1290 mile schedule between Southampton and Funchal plus a weekly link between Lisbon and Funchal which covered in four hours a journey which took thirty-six hours by boat.

Following the end of BOAC flying-boat operations Aquila took over many of their aircraft, including examples of the more extensively converted Sunderland known as the Sandringham Mk1 and several Solents. The first Aquila Solent G-AKNU was laid out as a forty-one-seater with a bar area and two decks connected by a spiral staircase.

A new service was opened on 7 July 1950, linking Southampton Water and St Aubin's Bay in Jersey. 'Hythe' flying-boats flew the route twice every Saturday throughout the summer and the service was re-instated for the 1951 season.

In December 1951 Solents took over the route to Funchal and the 'Hythes' were transferred to the Lisbon-Funchal link. The Funchal route was extended onwards to Las Palmas in 1952 and by 1954 the service had been upgraded to twice weekly to Funchal and weekly to Las Palmas.

On 1 May 1953 Aquila reduced their Southampton-Funchal fare from the winter level of £89.2.0 (£89.10) return to £59.10.0 (£59.50). This was an excursion fare which permitted a stay of up to twenty-one days on Madeira and was valid until 30 November. The growing success of this service meant that twice as many passengers were carried in May 1953 as in the same month the previous year. In a move designed to boost tourism still further the hoteliers on Madeira reduced their rates to as little as 18/9d (94p) per day for full board. Aquila also offered passengers a money-back weather guarantee whereby they refunded the full air fare plus an extra £40 to cover hotel and other expenses to any passenger who experienced more than half-an-inch of rain during a stay in July or August. The airline carried over 6,000 passengers during 1953.

On 3 June 1954 Aquila inaugurated another new service, this time to the Isle of Capri via Marseilles. This was the first ever direct air link from Britain to Capri and the journey took $8^3/4$ hours including a $1^1/2$ hour stop at Marseilles. The frequency was fortnightly at first but was soon increased to weekly from 1 July. By the end of the year Aquila's passenger total had reached 8,000.

Still more new destinations were added in 1955 with the opening of a weekly service to Santa Margherita on 4 June, followed by a weekly

Southampton-Genoa operation on the following day. Both of these services were timed to depart Southampton at the early time of 3 am in order to get passengers to their resort in time for breakfast and thus give them an extra day on holiday.

On 8 January 1956 Aquila began a fortnightly direct Southampton-Las Palmas service, although this did still involve a refuelling stop at Lisbon, and in June yet another new route was opened, to Montreux, where the aircraft landed on Lake Geneva.

By 1958 however the absence of a suitable replacement for the ageing Solents, coupled with intense competition from charter airlines using more versatile landplanes caused the demise of Aquila Airways. The service to Funchal was the last route to cease and with its closure on 30 September 1958 all British commercial flying-boat operations came to an end. The three surviving Solents, G-AHIN, G-ANYI and G-AOBL were transferred to an associate company Aerovias Aquilas, with the intention of restarting operations under Portuguese registry but the scheme fell through. All three aircraft were ferried to the Tagus Estuary near Lisbon and were beached. The hulls remained there for many years until corrosion rendered them beyond repair and they were eventually scrapped.

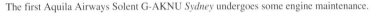

The first Aquila Airways Solent G-AKNU *Sydney* undergoes some engine maintenance.

Morton Air Services Airspeed Cons[...] G-AIOW at Croydon in the ear[...] 1950s. In the hangar behind can [...] seen an Avro Anson.

1530 hours on 15 August 1952. [...] Havilland Dove 2 G-AKJG stan[...] outside the terminal building [...] Croydon. The indicator on the contr[...] tower shows that Runway 24 is th[...] active one.

Chapter 3

The Decline of Northolt and Croydon

In common with many other Ministry of Aviation-owned airports both Northolt and Croydon provided amenities for the ever-growing number of spectators who came to watch the comings and goings in the 1950s. Public enclosures were open from 11 am until dusk during the summer and the admission charge in 1953 was 6d (2^1/$_2$p) for adults and 3d (1^1/$_2$p) for children. Pleasure flights and pony rides were among the attractions on offer.

Northolt was used by BEA and many foreign national carriers for European scheduled services. Among these was Aer Lingus, who introduced 'Starflight' night flights from Dublin on 15 June 1950. These services left Dublin at 10 pm and Northolt at forty and fifty-five minutes past midnight, with cheap fares on offer from £4.5.0 (£4.25) one way. BEA continued to expand their extensive Viking-operated route network throughout the early 1950s, introducing a three-times weekly service to Barcelona on 22 October 1950.

A new era in airliner speed and comfort began on 29 July 1950 when BEA commenced the world's first scheduled passenger services by turbo-prop aircraft, using the prototype Vickers Viscount G-AHRF for a two-week trial period between Northolt and Paris (Le Bourget). Fourteen revenue passengers and twelve guests were carried on the inaugural flight. The same aircraft operated on BEA's schedules to Edinburgh between 15 and 23 August 1950, the period of the Edinburgh Festival. These flights were the first UK domestic passenger services to be flown by turbo-prop airliner.

On 24 January 1951 the first commercial services were flown by BEA's 'Pionair' class Dakota conversions. These aircraft had been modified by Scottish Aviation at Prestwick for two-man cockpit operation and were equipped with built-in passenger airstairs. Each example was named after an aviation pioneer. The first service was a charter to Dublin for Smiths Instruments using G-ALYF 'RMA Pionair'. More development work towards the full introduction of Viscount services was carried out in mid-1951 by two of BEA's Dakotas which had been re-engined with Rolls-Royce Dart turbo-props. These aircraft were used on freight schedules. The first service, to Hanover on 15 August 1951, was the first commercial freight service by a turbo-prop aircraft.

In August 1951 BEA assessed the suitability of the new De Havilland Heron for use on the Channel Island routes. The prototype Heron G-ALZL was leased from the manufacturers and used for 34 trips between Northolt and Jersey during the period 4 August–2 September. Immediately following these trials another new type appeared at Northolt when 'Elizabethan' class Airspeed Ambassadors replaced the usual Vikings on some Paris schedules from 3 September. When the 'Elizabethan' fleet entered full BEA service however it was operated mainly from London Airport, with the Vikings and Dakotas serving on Northolt movements.

Scottish Airlines introduced two new destinations on 9 June 1951 when they began flying Dakotas into Northolt from Prestwick via RAF Burtonwood, which was mid-way between Manchester and Liverpool and was envisaged as a convenient airport for both these cities. This service was to remain in operation until February 1953.

On 19 November 1951 BEA began a mixed passenger/cargo flight to Hanover, using Vikings four times each week and on 20 April 1952 air services between Northolt and Manchester were re-introduced after a gap of four years. Once again BEA Vikings were used. During 1952 the high-density seating 'Admiral' class Viking conversions entered service with BEA and these made possible the introduction of new low fares such as a round trip to Paris for £9.15.0 (£9.75) return. Viking G-AMNJ operated the first of these services on 1 October and other Viking destinations introduced during 1952 included Basle from 2 May and an 'Admiral' class service to Helsinki for the duration of the Olympic Games in July.

Passengers board BEA Dakot G-ALXM at Northolt in the earl 1950s. The destination board at the to of the steps reveals the flight' destination to be Guernsey. Thi colour scheme was adopted by BE/ in 1950.

To cater for the growing holiday traffic to Spain BEA introduced a service to Palma on 15 May 1953. The journey by Viking took a total of 6 hours 10 minutes outbound and 6½ hours on the return leg, including a technical stop at Bordeaux in each direction. The fare was £21.15.0 (£21.75) single and £39.3.0 (£39.15) return.

During 1953 1.3 million passengers used BEA's services from Northolt.

1954 was to be the last year of airline operations from Northolt but there was a flurry of activity during the first half and the addition of a new operator with the transfer of Hunting-Clan's Newcastle-London service from Bovingdon on 1 April. The move was only temporary however and on 3 October the airline again relocated its London terminus, this time to London Airport. On 11 April BEA commenced Viking operations to Biarritz, initially via Bordeaux but direct from 28 May.

A railway strike resulted in an airlift of newspapers to the West Country between 18 and 29 May 1954. 531 tons of newspapers were carried aboard 170 night flights to Cardiff and Exeter. BEA organised the airlift and made ninety-seven flights with their own Vikings and Dakotas, the balance being flown by Airwork, Eagle Aviation, Hunting-Clan, Silver City and Transair.

On 30 October 1954 BEA operated the last commercial service from Northolt. This was a passenger schedule to Jersey by Dakota G-AHCZ. The airline then transferred its operations to London Airport, ending an eight-year association during which more than 300,000 aircraft movements had carried five million passengers. The last BEA aircraft to leave Northolt was a Viking on a positioning flight and the following day BEA retired the Viking fleet which had flown 65 million miles for them.

Croydon had been the principal airport for London and the operating base of the legendary Imperial Airways in the 1930s but the rapid developments in aircraft design during the war years had rendered it unsuitable for the new generation of heavier and faster post-war airliners. The lack of concrete runways and the presence of housing developments on all sides made expansion impracticable and the airfield was thus restricted to use by aircraft of Dakota size or smaller and was used principally for short-haul routes and charter flights. Two of the longest established residents were Olley Air Service and Morton Air Services.

Olley Air Service was founded as a charter operator at Croydon by Captain Gordon Olley in 1934. After World War Two the company resumed operations, initially with Rapides, later adding Airspeed Consuls and De Havilland Doves. The airline specialised in the provision of day-trip charters from Croydon to major race meetings throughout the UK. In 1949 they operated a summer service to Le Touquet which was reinstated for the 1950 season but dropped in 1951 in favour of routes to Weston-super-Mare and Bristol (Whitchurch) and from Bristol to Exeter, Newquay and Lands End. These services were all operated under BEA Associate Agreements. In 1952 the West Country operations ceased and a summer service to Guernsey and Jersey was flown instead.

In February 1953 Olley Air Service was taken over by Morton Air Services and many of the Olley aircraft became part of the initial fleet of Cambrian Air Services.

Morton Air Services had been based at Croydon since 1946 and like Olley Air Service they also made a speciality of charters to racecourses such as Doncaster, Aintree and Newmarket. They purchased modern equipment in the form of De Havilland Doves in 1948 and were to operate many of the type until 1969 when they finally disposed of their last three examples after 20 years as a Dove operator.

In the summer of 1951 Morton inaugurated scheduled services to Innsbruck, Le Zoute and Ostend. After the takeover of Olley Air Service in 1953 summer schedules were also flown to Guernsey, Jersey, Deauville and Le Touquet.

Another major operator based at Croydon was Transair Ltd., who had specialised in the operation of newspaper charter flights since 1948. By 1950 the destinations served by these flights from Croydon included Paris (Le Bourget), Brussels and the Channel Islands, with most flights being operated by Avro Ansons. In 1952 Transair was awarded another large contract, for the carriage of American newspapers from Frankfurt to Croydon for distribution to US armed forces stationed in Britain. A similar contract covered the import of the *Herald Tribune* from Paris into Croydon. By this time Transair was operating almost 3,000 newspaper flights annually and in 1953 Dakotas were acquired to replace the Ansons.

The Transair Ansons were also used for a rather unusual activity, the carriage of live lobsters from Benbecula in the Outer Hebrides to Croydon for onward distribution to Continental markets. At the height of the 1951 season two lobster flights were being made each day.

The new airport at Rotterdam was officially opened on 1 October 1956 and Morton Air Services became one of the first airlines to serve the airport, commencing services from Croydon on that day with Doves and their newly-acquired Herons. This was Morton's only year-round scheduled service.

On 18 March 1958 Captain Gordon Olley died and in accordance with his wishes his ashes were later scattered over Croydon Airport from a former Olley Air Service aircraft.

During 1958 Morton Air Services opened a weekly Croydon-Brawdy (Pembrokeshire) service. In 1959 the frequency was increased to twice-weekly and an optional stop at Swansea was introduced.

Croydon Airport was closed for flying on 30 September 1959. The last commercial service to arrive was a Morton Air Services Dove on a charter from Newmarket Racecourse which landed at 1720 hours and the last scheduled service departure was at 1839 hours when Morton Heron G-AOXL took off for Rotterdam. All of Morton's operations were then transferred to Gatwick Airport.

There were thirty-seven aircraft movements on the last day. The very last take-off was made by Mr Christopher De Vere in a Miles Gemini bound for Gatwick at 1946 hours and the airfield officially closed for operations at 2230 hours.

The mainstay of BEA's services from Northolt – the Vickers Viking. G-AJBR *Sir Bertram Ramsay* is pictured here.

1952 Olley Air Service advertisement for their air taxi service from Croydon.

BOAC Hermes 4 G-ALDM in flight near the Needles, circa 1950. The Hermes fleet served on African routes from 1950 until the end of 1954.

Chapter 4

The Growth of Heathrow

In 1950 all airline services at London Airport, as it was then called, used a collection of pre-fabricated single storey buildings along the perimeter of the Bath Road as the North Side Terminal Area. Building work was in progress however on what was eventually to become the Central Area complex, and excavation had begun on a tunnel beneath runway 10L/28R to link the Central Area with the outside world. Three runways were in service and radio and telecommunications, beacons and runway lights were all operational. Four hangars had been erected including a large one which Pan American Airways had shipped over in sections from the USA, and four more were under construction, including one for BOAC and a £2 million five-bay concrete complex for BEA. This would be 1,000ft long when completed and was intended as a home for the forthcoming Ambassador and Viscount fleets.

The airport was already the busiest in Europe, with seventeen companies operating scheduled services, and in 1950 523,357 passengers passed through aboard 37,746 aircraft movements. All this activity attracted 340,000 spectators to the airport during the year and to cater for their future needs a new public enclosure was under construction. Also visible were the beginnings of a two-storey reinforced concrete building which would become the new departure lounge and airline offices when BEA transferred their operations from Northolt Airport.

BEA operated their first scheduled flight from London Airport on 16 April 1950, a Vickers Viking service to Paris, but most of their flights still operated from Northolt and it would be October 1954 before the changeover was finally completed.

It was also in 1950 that BOAC introduced new standards of passenger comfort on their African routes with the entry into service of their new Handley Page Hermes 4 airliners. The route to Accra via Tripoli, Kano and Lagos was the first to benefit when Hermes equipment replaced the previous Avro Yorks on 7 August 1950. Next came the Nairobi route on 24 September. The four-times weekly Hermes operation replaced the former flying-boat service from Southampton Water and took twenty-seven hours to fly via Rome, Cairo and Khartoum, or $28^{1}/_{2}$ hours when an additional stop was made at Entebbe. Finally the Hermes fleet displaced the flying-boats on the run to Johannesburg from 7 November. These flights were operated in conjunction with South African Airways as the joint 'Springbok' service. Both airlines made three round-trips each week, the SAA schedules being flown by their Lockheed Constellation aircraft.

THE WORLD'S FIRST pure jet airline into service, the Comet Jetliner introd completely new era of passenger air transpo Powered by four D.H. Ghost 50 engines, ea veloping 5,000 lb. static thrust for take-off at r.p.m., the Comet is the fastest passenger in operation and cruises smoothly and easily m.p.h. true air speed. With a take-off we 105,000 lb., the maximum range is 3,860 mi flight, the absence of any sign of an engine, pr or other moving part, together with the rem quietness and freedom from vibration, give the of being fixed in, rather than travelling t space. On the flight deck, which carries a four, the simplicity of controls and instrumen immediately apparent. This simplicity reflec whole character of the Comet Jetliner. Ever of the interior has been designed to ensure ma comfort for the 36 passengers. The pressuri air-conditioned cabins are fitted with super-co able "Slumberseats"; over each seat is an ind beamlight; from the compact galley complim meals and meal-time drinks are served b stewards and a stewardess. When you tra Comet Jetliner, you get the best of both w the first experience of a new era of flying, wi same high standards of British service and ef enjoyed by B.O.A.C. passengers for the past 35

Passengers relax and enjoy efficient, courteous attention in the restful comfort of the Comet.

A 1951 BOAC promotional leaflet on their forthcoming Comet 1 services. The Comet 1 entered commercial service on 2 May 1952 but was withdrawn two years later after catastrophic in-flight failures.

On 2 August 1951 new salary scales were introduced for BEA and BOAC pilots. A Senior Captain First Class had his salary increased from £1500 p.a. to £2150 and a First Officer's remuneration went up from £750 p.a. to £1035, with annual increments of £30 up to a maximum of £1305.

At midnight on 8 October 1951 Their Royal Highnesses Princess Elizabeth and the Duke of Edinburgh boarded the BOAC Stratocruiser flagship *Canopus* for a flight to Dorval Airport, Montreal via Gander, Newfoundland at the start of their Canadian Tour. This was the first Royal Tour to depart from London Airport and also the first occasion that members of the British Royal Family had crossed the Atlantic by air. They returned home from Canada just before Christmas. On 31 January 1952 these same Royal personages set off from London Airport on another Royal Tour, this time to East Africa. His Majesty King George VI was at the airport to see them depart aboard BOAC Argonaut *Atlanta* for Nairobi via El Adem. Sadly, the tour was cut short by the death of the King a few days later and at 4.30pm on 7 February 1952 Her Majesty Queen Elizabeth II disembarked from the same aircraft at London Airport to set foot on British soil for the first time as Monarch.

KEY TO DIAGRAM: 1 Front passenger cabin ·
Main passenger cabin · 3 Rear baggage hold · 4 Men's
dressing room · 5 To men's toilet · 6 Ladies' toilet ·
Ladies' dressing room · 8 Main entrance and vestibule ·
Wardrobe · 10 Freight hold · 11 Stewardess · 12 Diplo-
matic mail locker · 13 Pantry · 14 Freight hold · 15 Navi-
gator · 16 Captain · 17 First Officer/Engineer · 18 Radio
officer · 19 Crew entry door · 20 Steward.

The flight deck
the Comet.

During 1952 BOAC was finding it difficult to maintain a sufficient complement of stewardesses for their expanding services and they advertised the posts at a salary level of £5.17.6 (£5.85) per week when flying and £2 per week when not. The advertisement attracted 800 applicants, out of which only three per cent were eventually accepted.

On 31 March 1952 BEA introduced the forty-seven-seater 'Elizabethan' class Airspeed Ambassador onto regular London-Paris schedules, initially on a twice-daily basis. These aircraft soon gained a reputation for passenger comfort and from 16 June they were used by BEA to re-introduce the luxury 'Silver Wing' lunchtime service to Paris, which had previously been operated by Imperial Airways from Croydon from 1927 until the outbreak of war. On the 'Silver Wing' service the 'Elizabethan' seating arrangement was reduced to forty and the duration of the simultaneous flights in each direction was deliberately extended so that passengers could enjoy a hot luncheon with champagne at their leisure.

At this point in the airport's development BEA had just one small hangar on the south side of the airfield and to taxi an aircraft from there through the massive Central Area construction site to the passenger terminal on the north side involved a circuitous journey of several miles. Despite these handicaps BEA's maintenance and overhaul work was gradually transferred from Northolt from 1952 onwards.

A momentous landmark in aviation history was established by BOAC on 2 May 1952 when they opened the world's first regular passenger service by a

G-ALZS RMS *Sir William Shakespeare,* one of BEA's fleet of elegant 'Elizabethan' class Airspeed Ambassadors.

jet airliner. The De Havilland Comet 1 G-ALYP flew the inaugural schedule from London to Johannesburg via Rome, Beirut, Khartoum, Entebbe and Livingstone and carried the thirty-six passengers over the 6,724 miles in an elapsed time of 23 hours 34 minutes. A Comet service to Colombo followed on 11 August, the 5,925 mile journey via Rome, Beirut, Bahrain, Karachi and Bombay taking 21 hours 35 minutes and slashing 12 hours 10 minutes off the scheduled time by the previous Argonaut equipment. To meet the competition from the jets South African Airways leased two Comets from BOAC for their 'Springbok' services. The Constellations thereby displaced were converted by SAA for Tourist Class services, a pointer to the coming trend towards lower fares. BOAC introduced their own Tourist Class Hermes services to Uganda, Kenya and the Sudan on 17 November 1952, offering savings of up to twenty-eight per cent off the regular fares.

Passengers board BOAC Comet G-ALYP for the world's first commercial jet airliner service on 2 May 1952. The thirty-six passengers were flown to Johannesburg in 23 hours 34 minutes.

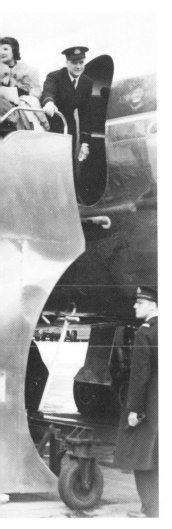

It was BEA's turn to be honoured with Royal patronage for the first time on 26 November 1952 when one of their 'Elizabethan' fleet carried HRH the Duke of Edinburgh from London to Malta.

Throughout 1953 the two major innovations of jet travel and Tourist Class fares were expanded in tandem, with the introduction of Comets onto more routes, releasing the older piston-engined types for use on reduced-fare services.

On 3 April BOAC inaugurated a weekly Comet service to Tokyo via Rome, Beirut, Bahrain, Karachi, Delhi, Calcutta, Rangoon, Bangkok, Manila and Okinawa. The scheduled flight time was thirty-six hours compared to eighty-six hours by Argonaut and night stops were eliminated. The frequency of this service was soon doubled to twice-weekly from 13 April. By this date the Comets were in service on nearly half of BOAC's route network and as a result the Corporation was able to utilise the Hermes and Argonaut fleets on new Tourist Class services to the Middle East, Singapore, Hong Kong, and Central Africa during the summer.

Typical of these new services was a weekly flight to Lusaka using a fifty-six-seat Hermes. Stops were made at Rome, Cairo, Khartoum, Entebbe and Nairobi and the total journey time including a night stop was 51^{1}/$_{2}$ hours. BOAC also offered a weekly Tourist service to Lod in Israel using Argonaut aircraft, also configured for fifty-six passengers. The journey entailed stops at Frankfurt and Rome and took 13 hours. About one third of BOAC's summer 1953 traffic was carried at reduced fares, which offered an average saving of twenty-five per cent.

From 1 April 1953 Tourist Class services were also introduced within Europe and from Europe to the Middle East. More than ninety per cent of BEA's seat capacity for the forthcoming summer would be on sale at the new lower rates. Other airlines were also offering low fares to Europe. Pan American Airways advertised their 'Rainbow' DC-6B service from London to Frankfurt for £14.19.0 (£14.95) one way or £26.19.0 (£26.95) return, or to Brussels or Amsterdam for £8.5.0 (£8.25) single and £14.17.0 (£14.85) return. SABENA were able to offer connections from London to Nice via Brussels for £27.10.0 (£27.50) return. Travel from London to Brussels was by Convair 240 with onward flights to Nice by the airline's brand-new DC-6Bs.

New standards of passenger comfort and speed on European routes were introduced by BEA on 18 April 1953 when they inaugurated the world's first sustained passenger service by turbo-prop airliner. On that date their Vickers Viscount 701 G-AMNY began services on the London-Rome-Athens-Nicosia route. The success of the Viscount was immediate. Furnished initially in a forty-seat all First Class layout the BEA Viscount 701 fleet made a net profit in its first year of operation of £301,000 after fully absorbing all introductory costs. For some five years to come there was no other turbine-powered airliner in operation on short and medium haul routes and BEA were eventually to operate twenty-seven Viscount 701s and forty-three of the larger 800 srs aircraft.

On 19 May 1953 BEA's Kensington Air Station in central London was closed down and the town terminal facilities transferred to the new Waterloo Air Terminal, which was officially opened by the Minister for Civil Aviation on 21 May.

BOAC retired their Hermes fleet on 1 October 1953 following the successful introduction of the Comet the previous year and Argonauts took over the Tourist Services to East Africa. All nineteen Hermes aircraft were offered for sale to the independent airlines but fears of redundancy among BOAC engineering staff led to a union ban on preparatory servicing on the aircraft and they were to remain cocooned on the south side of the airport for six months until the dispute was settled.

During 1953 London Airport was the venue for two unusual aviation events which were to stimulate public interest in the airport even more. On 8 May an Olympus-engined Canberra bomber took off from there to establish a new world altitude record of 63,668ft, and between 8 and 10 October the airport was the starting point for the London-Christchurch (N.Z.) Air Race. Prize money of £10,000 was on offer and in addition to three RAF and two RAAF Canberras in the Speed Section there was also a Transport Handicap

Section. Entrants in this category included an RNZAF Hastings C Mk.3, KLM DC-6A PH-TGA, which operated the flight as a commercial service carrying fare-paying passengers and special philatelic covers, and the prototype Viscount srs.700 G-AMAV which was entered by BEA and flown by a crew captained by Mr Peter Masefield. The Viscount carried race no.23 and was fitted with additional fuel tanks in the main cabin to give it a range of over 3,000 miles. The aircraft covered the distance of 11,975 miles in 40 hours 43 minutes at an average speed of 290 mph, stopping only at Bahrain, Colombo, the Cocos Islands and Melbourne. To coincide with the race, which was started by HRH the Duke of Gloucester, the new road tunnel into the Central Area was opened to the public for the first time.

On 2 December 1953 Air France introduced Viscounts onto regular Paris-London schedules. One of the first services to benefit from turbo-prop power was Air France's competitive response to the BEA 'Silver Wing' lunchtime flights. This was the 'Epicurean' service, which had until then been operated by Sud-Est Languedoc piston-engined airliners, and on which passengers were served with smoked salmon, caviare and unlimited champagne. Air France's Tourist class services were still operated by elderly Douglas DC-4s.

During 1953 more than one million passengers passed through London Airport, the first year this figure had been reached.

Following two catastrophic and initially unexplained in-flight structural failures BOAC was forced to ground its entire Comet 1 fleet and withdraw the aircraft permanently from service on 8 April 1954. All services to South America were suspended due to the acute shortage of aircraft and four of the cocooned Hermes aircraft lying at London Airport were re-commissioned and placed back into service on the East African routes until 4 December. South African Airways also placed their Constellations back onto First Class schedules. They were eventually superceded on the London run by DC-7Bs in 1959.

In 1954 BOAC's average fare was £80 and BEA's was £16.

A statue of pioneer aviators Alcock and Brown was unveiled at the airport on 15 June 1954 to commemorate the thirty-fifth anniversary of their first non-stop crossing of the Atlantic. The memorial was initially sited on the North Side apron but was later relocated to the Central Area when trans-Atlantic services were transferred there.

In August 1954 QANTAS replaced the L-749 Constellations used on their 'Kangaroo' service to London with larger and faster L-1049 Super Constellations, thereby reducing the journey time to forty-nine hours. The original Constellations were then converted to sixty-seat configuration and used on Tourist Class services to London until February 1955.

A bizarre accident occurred on 16 January 1955 when the crew of BEA Viscount 701 G-AMOK attempted to take off from a non-operational runway in poor visibility and struck a steel girder barrier which was in use as part of the Central Area construction work. Part of the Viscount's undercarriage and both port engines were torn off but fortunately only the captain and one passenger were injured. The aircraft was later rebuilt and sold in Venezuala.

airport employee stands by to remove passenger steps from SABENA nvair 240 OO-AWR in London port's Central Area on 7 July 1954. e destination board reassures sengers about the flight's destination. he background, a BEA 'Elizabethan' eives attention.

The first stage of the Central Area complex finally came into operation on 17 April 1955 when the Europa Building (renamed Terminal 2 in 1968) was opened for domestic and European services. BEA had been operating from the North Side apron since their last service from Northolt on 30 October 1954 but now they were the first airline to utilise the new terminal, with a departure to Amsterdam by their Viscount 701 G-AMOA. The terminal building, the new control tower and the Queen's Building offices and spectator terraces were all officially opened by HM the Queen on 16 December 1955. Also opened during that year was the first stage of BOAC's engineering base. Prior to the opening all maintenance and overhauls had been carried out at Filton, Bristol. Work commenced immediately on the second stage, which became known as the 'Britannia hangar' and came into service in 1957.

The West German national airline Deutsche Lufthansa resumed services to London on 16 May 1955 after a proving flight on 15 April which had included the first post-war landing in Britain of a German civil aircraft. The inaugural passenger services were operated by two Convair 340 aircraft which flew in from Munich via Frankfurt and from Hamburg via Dusseldorf.

A long-running cargo operation commenced on 23 July 1955 when Hunting-Clan Air Transport began their 'Africargo' service to Africa. The service, which initially originated in Manchester, flew weekly to East Africa and Salisbury, using Avro York freighters. Onward connections were offered to other East and Central African points. By the end of September the frequency had been doubled. Vikings were sometimes used in place of Yorks when loads were light. By 1957 the annual ton-mileage flown had trebled and two brand-new Douglas DC-6Cs were ordered. The first DC-6C schedule was flown on 14 December 1958. The service began to be profitable in 1959 and survived the merger of Hunting-Clan into British United Airways in 1960.

One of the Douglas DC-6As used by Hunting-Clan Air Transport on the 'Africargo' service to Central and East Africa was G-APNP, seen here with a cluster of Eagle Airways vans in the Central Area during 1960.

On 25 July 1955 the BEA Helicopter Unit began an experimental helicopter service between London Airport and the South Bank Heliport at Waterloo. S-55 Whirlwind G-ANUK, one of two purchased for £54,000 each, was used for this work and was modified to have a specially silenced engine and pontoon flotation bags for use in an emergency landing on the River Thames. The service ran until 31 May 1956. During that period 3,822 revenue passengers were carried and eighty-one per cent regularity achieved but there was never any hope of breaking even on the route. The fare charged for the seventeen-mile journey was 35/- (£1.75) and even if the maximum five passengers were carried on each of the eight daily services a loss of £322 would have been incurred.

BEA Westland-Sikorsky S-55 G-ANUK RMA *Sir Kay,* which was used for scheduled passenger services between London Airport and the South Bank Heliport at Waterloo during 1955 and 1956.

A new national carrier commenced operations into London in February 1956 when Air Ceylon started their weekly 'Sapphire' service from Colombo via Amsterdam. A leased KLM L-749 Constellation was used initially, fitted out with twelve 'Sleep Air' reclining sleeper seats and other seating for thirty-five Tourist Class passengers. An L-1049E Super Constellation was hired from KLM in place of the Constellation from November 1958 and this was in turn superseded by a KLM Electra turbo-prop in 1960.

A surprise visitor to London Airport on 22 March 1956 was Tupolev TU-104 CCCP-L-5400 of Aeroflot, making the first visit to Britain of a Soviet turbo-jet airliner. At that moment the TU-104 was the only jet airliner in service as the Comet 1s were grounded and the Comet 4 and the Boeing 707 were still at the design stage.

During 1956 over three million passengers used London Airport.

After a very protracted development period the Bristol Britannia entered BOAC service on 1 February 1957 when one of their 102 srs aircraft inaugurated the world's first long-haul turbo-prop air service, from London to Johannesburg. Stops were made at Rome, Khartoum and Nairobi and the scheduled journey time was 22 hours 50 minutes.

1957 was the year Icelandair commenced Viscount services to London and V.759 Viscount TF-ISN is seen parked outside the Pan American hangar on the airport's South Side. The distinctive Icelandair tail insignia has yet to be applied to this aircraft.

On 31 March 1957 the BEA fixed wing aircraft fleet consisted of twenty-six Viscount 701s, ten Viscount 802s, nineteen 'Elizabethan' class Ambassadors, thirty-eight 'Pionair' class Dakotas, three 'Islander' class Rapides, eight 'Pionair-Leopard' class Dakota freighters and three Herons. In addition the Helicopter Unit were using three S-55 Whirlwinds and single examples of the Bristol 171 and Bell 47B3.

The BEA West London Air Terminal at Cromwell Road in London opened on 6 October 1957, replacing the Waterloo Air Station

Mixed First and Tourist Class seating was offered aboard BEA flights for the first time on 1 May 1958 and during that year the steady introduction of turbo-jet and turbo-prop airliners led to the retirement from front-line service of two famous piston-engined types. BEA operated their last 'Elizabethan' service on 30 July when G-AMAF flew a Cologne-London sector. During their BEA service the 'Elizabethans' had flown thirty-one million miles and carried 2.43 million passengers. Reverting to their manufacturer's type name, the Ambassadors found a ready market among independent operators such as Dan-Air, Autair and BKS Air Transport. On 6 October BOAC Constellation G-ANTG flew into London from Abadan via Kuwait, Beirut and Rome on the Corporation's final Constellation passenger service.

Sharing the North Side tarmac together on 16 January 1958 were QANTAS Super Constellations VH-EAO and VH-EAP which were in the process of circling the globe in opposite directions on the airline's first round-the-world services. From October 1959 the Super Constellations were replaced by Boeing 707s which halved the Sydney-London flight time to twenty-four hours.

The new generation and the old meet in the North Side parking area on 14 November 1958. Comet 4 G-APDE was about to operate BOAC's 'Monarch' service to New York which had previously been flown by Stratocruisers such as G-ANTY in the background.

During 1958 London Airport retained its position as Europe's busiest airport. In the ten years since 1948 aircraft movements had increased from 23,000 to 116,000 and the number of passengers passing through the airport had grown from 280,000 to 3.5 million.

The QANTAS air hostess uniform, introduced in 1959 to coincide with the start of jet services.
A Boeing 707 tail fin forms the background to this picture.

BOAC introduced their own round-the-world service on 31 March 1959 when Britannia 312 G-OAVT left London to fly to Tokyo via the Atlantic and the Pacific. From Tokyo a Comet 4 completed the circumnavigation of the globe by flying to London through the Far East and the Middle East. Another Comet 4 operator at this time was Aerolineas Argentinas, whose Comets were used to inaugurate their turbo-jet services between London and South America on 20 May 1959. A twice-weekly schedule was provided, replacing the former DC-6 operation. BOAC Stratocruiser operations came to an end on 31 May 1959 when G-ANTY flew Accra-Kano-Barcelona-London.

By way of compensation another new airliner type was added to the London schedules when Caravelle F-BHRB inaugurated Air France's turbo-jet services from Nice and Paris to London on 27 July 1959. On 14 May that year BEA opened a London-Moscow service with Viscount 806s. Two days later Aeroflot commenced their reciprocal operation using TU-104s. Each airline contributed two round trips via Copenhagen each week. The First Class fare was £142.4.0 (£142.20) return and Tourist Class was £118.16.0 (£118.80) round trip. BEA was also offering package tours including accommodation for £120 per week.

25 August 1959 marked the fortieth anniversary of British scheduled international air services and the progress made during this period was evident on 18 October when Pan American Boeing 707 N719PA passed through London on the first ever all-jet round the world air service. Public interest in air transport was demonstrated by the visits of over one million spectators to the Roof Gardens above the Queen's Building and the Europa Building during the course of 1959.

On 1 April 1960 BEA became a scheduled jet operator with their inaugural Comet 4B service from Tel Aviv to London via Athens, using aircraft G-APMB. On the same day the Comet was introduced onto the Moscow route. Later that year BEA operated their last passenger service from London by piston-engined aircraft when Dakota G-AGZB flew a schedule to Birmingham on 31 October 1960. The aircraft was damaged on landing and the southbound return leg was cancelled. The Dakotas still continued on cargo-passenger services within Scotland until 1962.

Another BOAC piston-engined type went into retirement on 8 April 1960 when Argonaut G-ALHG flew into London from Abadan on the last service of the type for the Corporation. Like BEA's Elizabethans before them the BOAC Argonauts found a new lease of life with the independent airlines on charter flights.

17 May 1960 was the fortieth anniversary of KLM services into London and to mark the occasion their DC-8 PH-DCC flew in to London Airport carrying H. 'Jerry' Shaw, who had piloted the first service back in 1920, and Sir Frank Whittle who named the DC-8 after himself in a ceremony at the airport. On 17 December, the fifty-seventh anniversary of the first powered flight, BEA flew their first passenger service with a Vickers Vanguard. In the weeks to come Vanguards were substituted for smaller aircraft on an *ad hoc*

basis between London and Paris. In April 1960 BEA and Air France had introduced Tourist Class services on this route. No meals, refreshments or bar services were provided but the day return fare was reduced from £16.16.0 (£16.80) to £14.19.0 (£14.95). By 1962 BEA was offering inclusive tours to Paris based on scheduled services from London for £25.8.0 (£25.40) for eight days and fourteen-day tours by scheduled flights to Tangier for £66.19.0 (£66.95).

The Oceanic Building (known as Terminal 3 from 1968) opened for business on 16 November 1961 but initially it was reserved for BOAC flights only. Foreign long-haul carriers were not allowed to transfer their services across until 28 March 1962, on which date the North Side complex was finally closed to normal passenger services, although still used for VIP and cargo flights. One such VIP flight was the departure of HRH the Duke of Edinburgh on 9 February 1962 for a two-month tour of South America by a chartered BEA Herald turbo-prop.

BEA introduced purpose-built cargo aircraft into their fleet on 14 November 1961 when the first of their Argosy 102s entered service. By the following April they had replaced Dakotas and chartered Avro Yorks on services to Manchester, Copenhagen and Milan.

During July 1963 London Airport handled over one million passengers in a single month for the first time in its history. This was more than the total for the whole of 1953, only ten years earlier. To help cope with the demand the airport's first multi-storey car park, offering 1063 spaces, was opened on 20 August 1963.

An early 1960s view of the Centr. Area site, now occupied by Terminal Dominating the picture is Lufthans Viscount V.814D D-ANOL, and oth aircraft visible include BEA Dakota and Viscounts.

Two new British airliners entered scheduled service in 1964. On 1 April BEA's Trident 1s commenced full operations and on 29 April BOAC introduced the passengers' favourite, the Vickers VC-10, on the London-Lagos route.

A new spur road into the airport from the M4 motorway was opened on 23 March 1965 and on 10 June the development work that had been in progress since the early post-war years came to fruition with the world's first automatic approach and touchdown on a commercial airline service, by BEA Trident 1C G-ARPR using the Autoland system to land at London from Paris.

BEA aircrew salaries had increased somewhat by 1965 and a Viscount First Officer now earned £1300 pa. At the other end of the seniority scale a Trident or Comet Senior Captain was now paid £4700 pa.

The year ended with the withdrawal of another historic airliner type from first-line use. Comet 4 G-APDM flew into London from Auckland on 24 November 1965 at the end of BOAC's last scheduled Comet service.

A mid-1963 view of the Central Area aircraft stands from the spectators' terrace above the Europa Building. The foreground line-up comprises three BEA Vanguards and a Starways Viscount. Beyond them are Caravelles of Air France and Swissair, and in the distance is the site of today's Terminal 4.

BOAC L-049 Constellation G-AHEN operated on mainline trans-Atlantic routes from 1946 until it crash-landed at Filton in 1951. It was rebuilt and went on to serve with El Al Israel Airlines and Euravia.

Chapter 5

The Trans-Atlantic Struggle

At the beginning of the 1950s the premier airliner on the trans-Atlantic routes was the Boeing Stratocruiser. This derivative of the wartime B-29 bomber was faster and possessed a greater range than the Lockheed Constellations it superceded but it was more expensive to operate. This was acceptable in 1950 as all trans-Atlantic flights were in a one-class configuration with fares and levels of service comparable to (or possibly better than) today's First Class. At the beginning of the year both BOAC and Pan American Airways were operating Stratocruisers on services between London and the USA. BOAC had commenced operations on the London-Prestwick-New York (Idlewild) route in December 1949. The flagship of their fleet was named CALEDONIA in a ceremony at Prestwick at the beginning of 1950. Services were soon increased from three to five each week and then upgraded to daily, the displaced Constellation equipment being transferred to the London-Montreal route. The fare from London to New York and return in 1950 was $630 during the peak season and $466 off-peak.

On 1 October 1950 BOAC and Pan American were joined on the New York-London route by Trans World Airlines. The TWA service continued onwards to Frankfurt and was their first schedule through London, being acquired as part of a route-swapping agreement with the former incumbent American Overseas Airlines. TWA used L-049 Constellations for their flights. These aircraft were configured for forty-seven passengers. BOAC soon placed Stratocruisers onto the London-Montreal run, the first service by the type taking place on 23 April 1950. The following year Trans-Canada Air Lines began a reciprocal service from Montreal to London and onward to Paris. This operation was inaugurated on 1 April 1951, using Canadair DC-4M North Star aircraft.

The potential for luxury layouts aboard the spacious cabins of the Stratocruisers was used to good effect by both BOAC and Pan American on their De Luxe services in 1951. BOAC introduced their 'Monarch' service to New York on 1 March 1951, initially on a thrice-weekly basis but upgraded to daily from 1 May.

Passengers paid a small surcharge for the privilege of travelling in the widest cabin of any propellor airliner and enjoying the standard of service normally only found on the ocean liners of that period. Free cocktails preceded a dinner of caviare, turtle soup, cold Inverness salmon, spring chicken with Wiltshire bacon and peas, Hampshire strawberries with fresh double cream, cheese and fresh fruit. Champagne and liqueurs were complimentary and male passengers were presented with exclusive 'Monarch' ties. After dinner, passengers could descend a small staircase to the downstairs cocktail lounge for a nightcap before retiring for the night in sleeper berths which folded down from the cabin walls. A further small supplement was payable for the use of these berths which came complete with mattresses, blankets, pillows and linen sheets.

Pan American's rival Stratocruiser operations were the 'President' and 'President Special' services. A surcharge of $50 each way was levied and passengers were provided with sleeper berths and seven-course meals with champagne. Orchids and perfume were presented to the ladies and the gentlemen received complimentary cigars. There were five cabin attendants to attend to forty-seven passengers and it was even possible to hire a private two or four-berth stateroom in the forward portion of the cabin.

To counter this opposition TWA launched their own 'London Ambassador' de Luxe service on 8 April 1951. L-749 Constellations were used, furnished in an eighteen-berth sleeper layout.

Another new airline joined the battle for trans-Atlantic passengers on 16 May 1951 when El Al Israel Airlines commenced Tel Aviv-London-New York services with L-049 Constellations.

Stratocruiser G-AKGH *Caledonia*, which was used on BOAC's 'Monarch' de-luxe service to New York from 1 March 1951.

N6528C *Clipper Midnight Sun,* one of the Douglas DC-6Bs used by Pan American on their 'Rainbow' tourist-class services to the UK from May 1952.

A development that was to change the face of trans-Atlantic air travel took place on 1 May 1952 when the very first Tourist Class services between Europe and North America were operated. On this date Pan American inaugurated their 'Rainbow' service from London to New York with one of their new Douglas DC-6B aircraft, the *Clipper Liberty Bell.* The cabin was equipped with eighty-two seats in five-abreast configuration, compared to the fifty-two passengers four abreast First Class layout, but the same forty-inch seat pitch was retained. A complimentary meal and beverage service was provided but alcoholic drinks had to be paid for. The fares charged were $270 one way and $486 return, compared to $395 each way on First Class services. By June 1952 this service was also operating from Prestwick to New York. BOAC's competitive response, launched on the same day, was their 'Mayflower' service to the USA which was paralleled by the 'Beaver' service to Canada. BOAC used rather more elderly L-049 Constellations which had been converted from their previous forty-three-seat layout to carry sixty-eight Tourist Class passengers. TWA also converted some of their L-049 Constellations to a sixty-seat configuration for use on Tourist Class flights to London.

BOAC's trans-Atlantic load factors in 1952 were 65 per cent in First Class and 67 per cent in Tourist Class. This compared with 68.7 per cent and 68 per cent respectively on Pan American and 63.1 per cent and 85.5 per cent on Trans-Canada Air Lines' services to Canada.

Tourist Class services across the Atlantic continued to expand during 1953. TWA added two more flights each week to their London-New York 'Sky Tourist' service, placing it on a daily basis and giving the airline a total of eleven trans-Atlantic trips each week. Pan American continued to offer their 'Rainbow' service and in October 1953 the fare from London to New York was £98.5.0 (£98.25) one way and £151.16.0 (£151.80) return. This fare was increased to £176.16.0 (£176.80) return in the peak season. The equivalent fares from Prestwick were £92.3.0 (£92.15) one way and £140.18.0 (£140.90) return low season or £165.18.0 (£165.90) high season.

On 28 October 1953 SABENA Belgian World Airlines inaugurated the first ever scheduled air service from the north of England to North America when they commenced their 'Manchester Premier' service from Manchester to New York. This all Tourist Class service originated and terminated in Brussels and was operated by DC-6B aircraft on a weekly basis. The DC-6B OO-CTH flew the inaugural service out of Manchester via Gander and arrived back at Manchester on the morning of 30 October after a non-stop flight of 11 hours 20 minutes. BOAC were not to offer flights from Manchester to the USA until 7 May 1954 when they opened a London-Manchester-Prestwick-New York Stratocruiser service. Even then they did not compete directly with SABENA as they did not introduce Tourist Class until 24 May 1955.

SABENA DC-6B OO-CTH starts its engines for the inaugural 'Manchester Premier' service to New York on 28 October 1953.

TWA L-1049G Super Constellation N7106C is provisioned during turn-round at London Airport's North Side in 1956/7. Beneath the tail a period catering vehicle loads supplies for the return leg.

Trans-Canada Air Lines were also expanding their route network from the UK and on 1 November 1953 they commenced services with North Star aircraft from London and Prestwick to Toronto. Their London-Montreal schedules were upgraded to more modern equipment on 14 May 1954 when L-1049 Super Constellations were placed onto the route.

TWA also introduced Super Constellations on the North Atlantic from 1 November, with a Washington-London service that was flown with forty-nine-seater L-1049Gs.

The load factors for the competing airlines in 1955 were: BOAC 64.1 per cent First and 63.4 per cent Tourist; Pan American 71.4 per cent First and 64.9 per cent Tourist; and TWA 71.6 per cent First and 70.55 per cent Tourist. Trans-Canada's First Class load factor to Canada had increased significantly to 72.9 per cent but Tourist had dropped to 76.7 per cent.

Cargo loads had also been increasing steadily over the years and on 19 February 1955 the first trans-Atlantic all-cargo scheduled service was inaugurated. Perhaps surprisingly this was not routed through London and was not operated by either a British or American company. Instead, it was Swissair Douglas DC-4 HB-ILU that carried out flight SR970 from Zurich and Basle to Manchester and onwards to New York via Shannon and Gander. British independent airline Airwork Ltd. followed this on 1 March 1955 with their own London-Manchester-Prestwick-Gander-Montreal-New York service. Initially, leased Transocean Airlines DC-4s were used. DC-6As soon superseded these but Airwork terminated the service in December.

Until the mid-1950s the strong headwinds encountered on westbound trans-Atlantic services had necessitated a refuelling stop at Gander and often another at Shannon or Prestwick as well but with the introduction of modern types such as the Douglas DC-6B it was sometimes possible to omit these. On 28 June 1954 a SABENA DC-6B made the first non-stop flight from Manchester to New York, taking 12 hours 56 minutes for the crossing. In 1956 Pan American introduced the Douglas DC-7C onto their trans-Atlantic routes. This was the first airliner capable of crossing the Atlantic non-stop in both directions and it brought London within 12 hours flying time of New York. Pan American's DC-7Cs entered service on 1 June 1956. They could seat ninety-one passengers in the all-Tourist layout. SABENA also used the type to replace DC-6Bs at the end of 1956 and during the year another new carrier began to offer trans-Atlantic flights from Manchester, this was the German airline Lufthansa, who inaugurated their 'Manchester Mid-Western' service to Montreal and Chicago via Shannon on 23 April 1956. L-1049G Super Constellations were used on the twice-weekly schedule which transited Manchester en route from Hamburg and Dusseldorf. At the end of the year though the service was suspended due to runway operating limitations at Manchester.

BOAC had intended to gain a competitive edge over its rivals by placing Bristol Britannia 312 turbo-props onto the North Atlantic routes in 1956 but delays in the delivery of these aircraft resulted in the airline acquiring a fleet of DC-7Cs as a stop-gap measure. On 11 November 1956 one of these machines on a proving flight covered the distance from London to New York non-stop in the record time of 10 hours 40 minutes and on 6 January 1957 the DC-7Cs entered commercial service on the 'Monarch' London-New York schedules. Although the 'Monarch' trade name had been retained for BOAC's premier trans-Atlantic routes the emphasis was now changing from leisurely luxury travel to speed of crossing as the trans-Atlantic passenger war hotted up. From 10 March 1957 the DC-7C flights continued onwards from New York to San Francisco and on 1 April the aircraft were used to compete with SABENA's machines on the Manchester-New York route. They were also employed on a new BOAC service from Manchester to Montreal, replacing the former Lufthansa schedules.

TWA introduced their answer to the DC-7Cs on 1 June 1957 when Lockheed L-1649A 'Jetstream Starliners' entered service on the London-New York route, carrying seventy-four passengers in an all-Tourist configuration.

The extended range of the latest generation of trans-Atlantic airliners was demonstrated on 10 September 1957 when Pan American inaugurated San Francisco-London-Paris DC-7C flights on the Polar 'Great Circle' routing. By taking this short cut over the Arctic it became possible to reduce the San Francisco-London flying time to under eighteen hours non-stop. On the following day the aircraft returned to San Francisco via Seattle with a refuelling stop at Frobisher Bay, Baffin Island. Two days later a similar

DC-7C operation from London to Los Angeles and San Francisco via Frobisher Bay was launched.

Not to be outdone TWA used their L-1649A Starliners to open their own London-Los Angeles Polar route on 30 September 1957 and followed this up on 2 October with a Polar service to San Francisco which was scheduled to cover the 4890 miles in 23 hours 19 minutes. In March 1958 however a TWA Starliner with eighteen passengers and ten crew aboard flew London-San Francisco non-stop in the record time of 19 hours 5 minutes.

It was 1960 before BOAC commenced their own Polar services, from London to Los Angeles with Boeing 707 jets, but shortly before the end of 1957 they began the first scheduled trans-Atlantic services by turbine-powered aircraft with the much-delayed entry into service of the Britannia srs 312s. On 19 December Britannias began to replace DC-7Cs on the London-New York route and from May 1958 they also took over on the services to San Francisco. These aircraft were very popular with passengers and their quiet and smooth handling earned them the nickname 'The Whispering Giants'.

Another major step towards bringing trans-Atlantic air travel within the reach of most people came on 1 April 1958 with the introduction of Economy Class fares. These fares were approximately twenty per cent cheaper than even Tourist Class, Pan American's Economy Class return fare to New York being set at $463.60 compared to $567 in Tourist and $783 in First Class. The seat pitch in the DC-7Cs was reduced to thirty-four inches, allowing 104 passengers to be carried instead of ninety-one in the Tourist Class layout. The number and composition of in-flight meals was strictly regulated by the International Air Transport Association.

More Canadian destinations became accessible from London on 28 May 1958 when Trans-Canada Air Lines launched their 'Hudson Bay' service to Gander, Winnipeg and Vancouver, again using Super Constellations.

The race to be the first with a pure-jet service across the Atlantic was narrowly won by BOAC on 4 October 1958 when they inaugurated Comet 4 operations. Simultaneous crossings in each direction were made on that date, with Comet G-APDC flying London-New York in 10 hours 22 minutes including a refuelling stop at Gander. Sister aircraft G-APDB flew non-stop from New York to London in the record time of 6 hours 11 minutes. The two aircraft passed each other approximately 300 miles apart in mid-Atlantic and wireless messages were exchanged between BOAC's Chairman on the westbound flight and their Managing Director on the other. The service was weekly at first but was increased to daily from 13 November after some schedule disruptions caused by a strike were resolved.

Only three weeks or so later Pan American also became a trans-Atlantic jet operator when their Boeing 707-121s entered service, initially on the New York to Paris via Gander route. Their first 707 had been delivered on 15 August 1958. The aircraft were furnished with eighteen First Class and 117 Economy Class seats, no Tourist Class seating being provided on any of Pan American's jets. The extra speed and capacity of the 707s meant that each one was able to do the work of three DC-7Cs.

BOAC were the first operator to provide pure-jet flights to Canada, their Comet 4s entering service on a weekly London-Montreal schedule on 19 December 1958. Britannia turbo-props were introduced in place of DC-7Cs on the Manchester-Montreal route from 16 April 1959.

To gain extra revenue from those passengers taking advantage of the much faster jet schedules and perhaps to encourage others to patronise those services still using propellor aircraft a jet surcharge was introduced on North Atlantic fare tariffs on 1 April 1959. The surcharge was set at $15 one way for Tourist and Economy Class and $20 for First Class and De Luxe services.

Not all airlines had jet aircraft in front-line service at this time and TWA relied on their Starliners to open the first non-stop Chicago-London service on 5 June 1959. The weekly eastbound schedule took 13 hours 10 minutes for the journey. In August the Starliners also took over the westbound service and flew the route non-stop in 15 hours 50 minutes. On 24 November 1959 however TWA introduced Boeing 707s onto the New York route and the Starliners' days were numbered.

There was however one airline which was to continue to use propeller-driven aircraft on the trans-Atlantic route until the latter half of the 1960s. This was Loftleidir Icelandic Airlines, who had commenced services from Glasgow to New York via Keflavik in 1956 with unpressurised DC-4s. The route was extended southwards to London in 1957 and in December 1959 pressurised DC-6Bs replaced the DC-4s. As Loftleidir's flights used non-jet equipment and included a compulsory stop in Iceland en route they were allowed to offer fares which were approximately sixteen per cent lower than their competitors' and their services were consistently popular with those passengers who were prepared to take a little longer to reach their destination and to save quite a lot of money by doing so.

On 1 March 1960 BOAC began serving Toronto with Comet 4s from London and on this date a revenue pooling arrangement with TCA came into effect.

Another new jet type came into service on the North Atlantic on 27 April 1960 when Pan American operated their first New York-London flight with Douglas DC-8 equipment. This was also Pan American's very first scheduled DC-8 service and aircraft N803PA performed the inaugural flight. The DC-8 fleet had been ordered by Pan American as a precaution against any introductory problems with the Boeing 707s and both types were to be seen operating the airline's flights into London for some years to come.

BOAC had meanwhile taken delivery of their first Boeing 707s, which were destined to take over the North Atlantic schedules from the Comets which were too small and had insufficient range for competitive operation on these routes. The first 707 service was flown from London to New York on 27 May 1960 and within a few months the Comets had been withdrawn completely from the North Atlantic, the last service being flown from New York to London on 16 October. Pure-jet equipment also came into operation on the Manchester-New York route, the first scheduled Boeing 707 flight being made by a SABENA aircraft on 20 April 1960. BOAC responded to

the competition by introducing 707s in place of Britannias from October. Eventually SABENA were forced off the route altogether and their last service was flown on 31 March 1964.

1960 was the first year in which more passengers crossed the Atlantic by air than by sea. Air traffic was up by twenty-three per cent whilst sea traffic declined by fourteen per cent.

On 28 May 1960 Trans-Canada Air Lines had celebrated the first visit of one of their new DC-8 jets to London by establishing a new Montreal-London speed record of 5 hours 44 minutes 2 seconds. This was a route-proving flight and the following day the same DC-8 flew from London to Prestwick in fifty-seven minutes to make the first visit of a DC-8 to this airport. After these proving flights TCA commenced scheduled DC-8 services from London with a flight to Montreal on 1 June 1960. From this date the DC-8 flights were placed on a daily basis.

Some of BOAC's redundant DC-7Cs were converted to DC-7F freighters in 1960 and on 3 December one of them opened BOAC trans-Atlantic all-cargo operations with a flight from New York to Prestwick. A week later a London-New York via Manchester, Gander and Montreal DC-7F service was inaugurated.

Propellor aircraft were also still in regular passenger service across the Atlantic at this time, on the low-fare services of Loftleidir. In the early 1960s they purchased five Canadair CL-44 turbo-props to replace their DC-6Bs. In 1964 these aircraft were stretched by 15 feet to become CL-44Js (or Rolls-Royce 400s, as the airline called them, referring to their Rolls-Royce Tyne engines). This modification increased the seating capacity from 160 to 189 and made them the largest aircraft on the North Atlantic route when they entered service on 29 May 1964.

In an attempt to profit from the shift from sea travel to air travel the Cunard Steamship Company formed a joint company with BOAC to operate North Atlantic services. The new airline was named BOAC-Cunard and seventy per cent of the shares were held by BOAC. The airline's first 707 service left London on 24 June 1962 bound for New York and Bermuda via Manchester and Prestwick.

The massive increase in traffic during the early 1960s enabled Pan American to reduce both First and Economy fares in April 1964. The new Economy fare to New York was $210, compared to the 1952 Tourist fare of $270 and a new fourteen to twenty-one day excursion fare of $300 return was introduced.

In April 1964 BOAC replaced the Britannias on the Manchester-Montreal route with Boeing 707s.

The stretched Super VC-10 version of the popular Vickers VC-10 entered service on the North Atlantic on 1 April 1965, operating BOAC's 'Monarch' service from London to New York and Bermuda. Initially the service operated six times each week, continuing onwards from New York to San Francisco instead of Bermuda once a week. The frequency was soon increased to fifteen trans-Atlantic flights per week and the rear-engined VC-10s were to win many passengers away from the 707s and DC-8s of their competitors with their quiet cabin environment and smooth handling. They were to remain the most popular aircraft with trans-Atlantic passengers throughout the 1960s and up to the beginning of the 'Jumbo Jet' era.

BOAC DC-7C G-AOII taxies through the Central Area at London Airport in the early 1960s. In the background are BEA Dakotas and Viscounts.

G-AJBI, one of the many Morton A Services Doves, pictured with a Dako at their Gatwick Airport maintenan base.

Chapter 6

The Rebirth of Gatwick

During 1950 over 11,000 passengers and 169 tons of freight passed through Gatwick Airport. One of the contributory factors to this encouraging result was the introduction in May 1950 of a BEA Rapide service to Alderney. The next two years however were to see traffic decline to less than a quarter of the 1950 figures.

There were some encouraging signs though. In 1951 the BEA Experimental Helicopter Unit moved to Gatwick from its previous base at Peterborough and commenced experimental mail and passenger services with a fleet of three Sikorsky S-51s and two Bell 47s. In 1953 two Bristol 171s were delivered to the Unit. These were the first British-designed helicopters to be used by BEA, who were to maintain a helicopter base at Gatwick throughout the 1950s and 60s.

Two new services were opened during 1953. Silver City Airways commenced a short-lived car ferry service to Le Touquet on 15 April and Jersey Airlines inaugurated their own service to Alderney using De Havilland Herons. This service was to remain in operation until Gatwick was closed for redevelopment in 1956. Thanks to these new schedules the 1953 traffic figures reached 14,000 passengers and 930 tons of freight.

In 1954 a government White Paper was published stating the intention to develop Gatwick as London's second airport. By January 1955 Treasury authority had been granted for the purchase of the necessary additional land. A contract was awarded for the diversion of the A23 trunk road and by the end of the year work had commenced. On 31 March 1956 the airport was closed to all air traffic except the BEA helicopter unit and construction work began in earnest.

A new runway was constructed across the site of the former Gatwick Racecourse, which had been requisitioned during the war, and the River Mole was diverted under the runway through a system of culverts. A brand new terminal building was erected, incorporating the first passenger pier at a European airport and the railway station was moved to a site alongside the terminal. When the work was completed in 1958 Gatwick became the first airport in the world to combine air, mainline rail and trunk road transportation facilities under one roof.

The first aircraft to land at the rebuilt airport was a Transair Viscount inbound from Gibraltar on a trooping flight on 30 May 1958. The official opening ceremony did not take place however until 9 June. On that date HM The Queen and HRH Prince Philip flew in aboard a Heron of the

Queen's Flight. After the inauguration the first official departure was made by a BEA Dakota which had been chartered by Surrey County Council to carry a party of dignitaries to Jersey and Guernsey. Shortly after that the first scheduled airline movement was provided by a Jersey Airlines Heron, also bound for the Channel Islands.

Despite the ultra-modern facilities on offer the airport authorities still had trouble in attracting more operators to use Gatwick. Airlines were reluctant to use the airport as a bad weather alternate to London Airport because of the expense involved and would often cancel flights rather than risk a possible diversion. During 1958 the only new company to establish a base at the airport was Transair who moved from Croydon, which was not suitable for the operation of their new Viscount fleet. Transair constructed their own £$^1/4$ million maintenance facility which incorporated a special Viscount maintenance dock with hydraulically operated retracting pits. From Gatwick they flew a mixture of newspaper, trooping and inclusive-tour flights as well as a scheduled service to Jersey.

The airport suffered a mauling at the hands of the British weather on 5 September 1958 when a severe storm tore off part of the Transair hangar roof and the River Mole flooded parts of the terminal building. Despite these teething troubles Gatwick still handled 186,172 passengers in the seven operational months of 1958 and this was six times any previous whole-year total.

Transair were joined at Gatwick in 1959 by Morton Air Services who transferred their operating base on the closure of Croydon Airport. Morton's fleet of Doves and Herons operated scheduled services to Rotterdam, Swansea and the Channel Isles. On 8 June 1959 Sudan Airways became the first foreign scheduled operator into Gatwick. A leased Airwork Viscount was used on a weekly schedule from Khartoum via Cairo, Athens and Rome. Other new operators that year included Air Links with a single Dakota, African Air Safaris with two Vickers Vikings, Pegasus Airlines also with Vikings and Derby Airways with Dakotas. These airlines were principally concerned with inclusive-tour charters to Mediterranean resorts. The passenger total for 1959 reached 368,000 but the new terminal facilities were still very under-utilised.

By the end of 1960 however the passenger figure had grown to 470,000, due mainly to the arrival of two major new operators. On 14 June Overseas Aviation transferred their base from Southend Airport to a new purpose-built hangar at Gatwick. This building, which was opened by the Parliamentary Secretary to the Minister of Aviation, had a clear span of 150 feet and was thirty-three feet high. It cost £300,000 to build and at the time was the largest clear span building in the UK. Overseas operated their large fleet of Vikings and Argonauts on inclusive-tour flights from Gatwick to a large number of resort destinations.

Another major new airline was born on 1 July 1960 when Hunting-Clan Air Transport, Airwork Ltd., Air Charter Ltd., Transair, Morton Air Services and Olley Air Service merged to form British United Airways. Mr Freddie

Laker was appointed Managing Director of the new combine which was the largest British independent airline and was based at Gatwick. A fleet of Viscounts, Britannias, DC-6s, DC-4s and Dakotas was employed on scheduled services to Gibraltar, Le Touquet, Jersey, Guernsey and several African destinations. BUA was to continue to expand and to play a major role in placing Gatwick firmly on the airline map. This was demonstrated in 1961 when the airline became the first in the world to order the BAC 1-11 short haul jet, and again at the beginning of 1962 when they opened in conjunction with British Railways a city centre check-in facility above the platforms at Victoria Station in London. Passengers were then able to check their luggage in at Victoria and it would be transferred for them from the train to the aircraft at Gatwick while they went straight to the departure lounge.

British United Bristol 170 MK 31 G-ANMF was equipped with fifty-one seats and used on rail-air services from Gatwick to the Continent until 1967. In the distance are the Morton Air Services and Air Couriers hangars.

From 1961 onwards BEA attempted to transfer some of their services to Paris and other European destinations from London Airport to Gatwick but these attempts were unsuccessful as their foreign counterparts would not do likewise and by the spring of 1963 only their Channel Island services still operated from Gatwick.

However the end of 1961 saw the establishment of another champion of Gatwick in the form of Caledonian Airways. Their first aircraft was a 104-seat DC-7C which they leased from SABENA for £5,000 per month. This aircraft performed Caledonian's very first revenue-earning operation in November 1961 when it flew a Barbados-Gatwick immigrant charter on behalf of London Transport, carrying ninety-three men and two women to employment on London's buses and underground railway system.

During 1962 Air Couriers Ltd. opened a large maintenance facility at the southern end of the airport to provide contract maintenance and overhauls for airline and corporate owners of aircraft up to DC-7C or Super Constellation size. That same year work commenced on doubling the size of the terminal building as well as adding two more passenger piers and extending the runway to 8,200 feet. Another new feature that year was soon to become a familiar sight to motorists passing the airport along the Brighton road. This was the fuselage of former Silver City Airways Hermes 4 G-ALDG, which BUA had purchased for use as a cabin staff training mock-up. It was repainted in their colours and positioned outside their maintenance area adjacent to the main road.

Traffic figures at the airport around this time received a useful boost from the many affinity group charter flights operated to the USA by Caledonian Airways and American supplemental carriers such as Capitol Airways. Special reduced group fares were available on such charters provided that all the passengers were members of some form of sporting or social association. A contributor to this book travelled on a typical flight in August 1962. The DC-7C aircraft was operated by Riddle Airlines of the USA and flew from Gatwick to Gander, Newfoundland in ten hours. After a refuelling stop the onward leg to New York took a further five hours. With the help of a tailwind the return crossing to Gatwick was flown non-stop in twelve hours. The return fare was £60.

In the spring of 1965 BUA took over the BOAC South American route network, commencing with a twice-weekly VC-10 service to Santiago in Chile. They followed this on 9 April 1965 with the world's first commercial BAC 1-11 service, from Gatwick to Genoa. G-ASJJ operated the inaugural flight.

The extensions to the terminal facilities and runway were officially opened on 22 June 1965 by the Minister of Aviation, Mr Roy Jenkins. Passengers for the financial year 1965/6 totalled 1.4 million. Gatwick could justifiably claim to be London's second airport in every sense.

ACE Freighters used L-749 Constellation G-ALAK on cargo services from Gatwick during 1965.

Dan-Air used Airspeed Ambassadors on both scheduled services and holiday charters from Gatwick. G-AMAG taxies onto its stand at the southern passenger pier in the mid-1960s.

Passengers boarding BEA Viking G-AIVB at Glasgow (Renfrew) Airport in June 1954 display
the latest fashions in travel wear.

Chapter 7

Regional Scheduled Services

In 1949 there were ninety-three private airlines registered in Britain as well as the state corporations BEA and BOAC, but by 1959 this number had dwindled to forty-four. Most of the companies in existence at the beginning of the 1950s relied on the operation of holiday charter flights for their livelihood and this resulted in considerable over-capacity and many financial failures. From May 1948 until 1960 the independents were permitted to operate domestic scheduled services, but only under BEA Associate Agreements which effectively restricted them to those routes which BEA had no wish to operate with their own aircraft. International services to the major capitals of Europe were usually allocated to the state airline BEA as a matter of government policy. Those private airlines which survived throughout the 1950s were generally those which had the financial backing of large shipping interests, such as Airwork, Britavia, Hunting-Clan and Skyways.

In 1960 however the Civil Aviation (Licencing) Act abolished the monopoly rights of the state airlines to scheduled services and established the Air Transport Licencing Board to award route licences and fix domestic fares. The Act was still a disappointment to the independent sector in some ways though. No sudden or far-reaching changes to the existing pattern of operations were envisaged, the private airlines were only allowed to operate a limited frequency on routes in direct competition with BEA, and only one British carrier was permitted on each international route, with preference being given to the state corporations. Despite these handicaps however the independent airlines managed to expand their scheduled services in tandem with the rapid growth of BEA and BOAC throughout the period covered by this book.

For convenience this summary of scheduled services out of regional airports has been divided into two geographical sections.

Regional Scheduled Services — North

At the beginning of the 1950s BEA's Scottish route network was based at Renfrew Airport,GLASGOW, which had been used during the war as an assembly plant for American-built warplanes delivered to Glasgow by sea. The airfield was greatly extended in 1942 for this purpose, acquiring three new hangars and two all-weather runways which were to prove a valuable asset when full civil operations resumed in 1945.

BEA's mainline routes to London and other major cities were operated by Dakotas and it was one of these aircraft which inaugurated a new service to

Paris via Manchester in April 1950. The same year a taste of the future shape and sound of airline travel was provided by the prototype Vickers Viscount G-AHRF which visited the airport on a proving flight on 1 August. This was the first visit of a turbo-prop airliner to Renfrew.

Services to the Highlands and Islands were mainly operated by 'Islander' class Rapides, which were also used on the Scottish Air Ambulance Service, provided by BEA. In 1950 BEA had a total of nineteen Rapides, which were used on Channel Isles and Scilly Isles services as well as the Scottish routes. On 30 September 1952 however the Rapides were replaced by Dakotas on all the Scottish routes except the run to Tiree and Barra (where the aircraft landed on the beach at low tide) and the Air Ambulance flights. The Rapides soldiered on with these services until February 1955 when two Heron 1Bs were delivered to Renfrew and were placed onto the Glasgow-Tiree-Barra route. The first Heron-operated Air Ambulance flight took place on 4 March 1955.

By this time BEA's Dakotas had been converted by Scottish Aviation at Prestwick into the 'Pionair' class configuration. This featured a new thirty-two-passenger layout, a revised cockpit for two-crew operation and built-in airstairs. Certain examples were equipped for mixed cargo/passenger operation and in this version they were known as the 'Pionair-Leopard' class. A total of thirty-eight Dakotas were converted into these two variants.

For the winter of 1952/3 BEA introduced special £8 weekly return fares on the routes from Glasgow and Edinburgh to London. In April 1953 their lowest fares on these routes averaged 2³/₄d (approx 1.25p) per mile, which BEA claimed was the cheapest rate in the world.

A new routing Glasgow-Edinburgh-Birmingham-Northolt was inaugurated on 19 April 1953. More modern equipment in the form of Vickers Vikings had been placed onto services from Glasgow to Northolt, Birmingham and Manchester, and turbo-prop power came to Scottish routes on a permanent basis on 2 October 1953 when the 'Clansman' First-Class Viscount service between Glasgow and London was introduced. 'Clansman' departures were ceremonially seen off from Glasgow with a salute from the BEA Duty Officer and a piper playing. Two days after the 'Clansman' inaugural BEA began to use Viscounts on Tourist-Class services to Scotland and that summer Viscounts were also used by Aer Lingus on their Glasgow-Dublin route, covering the distance in 1hr 20mins.

On 26 November 1954 a new terminal building at Renfrew was officially opened by the Minister of Transport and Civil Aviation. The original building was then taken over by Scottish Aviation in connection with their contract for the overhaul of Royal Canadian Air Force jet fighters. Runway limitations caused the transfer of this work to Prestwick in 1959/60.

Throughout the 1950s trans-Atlantic services were operated from Renfrew via Reykjavik, and these flights also provided a regular link between Scotland and Iceland and Scandinavia. On 20 October 1956 Loftleidir (Icelandic Airlines) began a weekly Reykjavik-Glasgow-Stavanger service and the following year the other Icelandic airline Flugfelag Islands (soon to be known as Icelandair) introduced Viscounts on their Reykjavik-Glasgow-

Copenhagen service. The inaugural Viscount flight took place on 3 May 1957 and three days later the Viscounts also came into operation on the Reykjavik-Glasgow-London route.

Turbo-prop aircraft of a different kind began to use Renfrew on 15 December 1958 when Aer Lingus inaugurated their first Fokker F-27 Friendship route, from Dublin to Glasgow.

From 20 December 1960 BEA began to substitute Vickers Vanguards for Viscounts on some London-Renfrew flights but problems were experienced in operating this very large turbo-prop airliner into Renfrew's restricted runway and the decision was taken to develop nearby Abbotsinch as the new airport for Glasgow. Abbotsinch was originally an RAF base before its transfer to the Navy as HMS *Sanderling* in 1943. The airfield was closed in 1963 for work to commence on its conversion to a civil airport.

BEA still maintained its claim to offer the world's cheapest air fares per mile with the introduction of off-peak night services from London to Glasgow (and Edinburgh and Belfast) on 1 November 1961. These were to be augmented on 1 April 1963 by stand-by fares on these routes at one-third of the normal rates.

The first visit to Renfrew by a pure-jet airliner was made by Iberia Caravelle EC-ARI on 28 April 1962. On the following day Cambrian Airways inaugurated a Glasgow-Manchester-Bristol-Cardiff Dakota service. BEA's Dakotas were finally retired after 'Pionair-Leopard' class aircraft G-ALTT flew the last Islay-Campbeltown-Glasgow Dakota service on 19 May 1962. Their replacements on the Scottish routes were three Handley Page Herald 101s which had been purchased by the Ministry of Aviation on behalf of BEA. These were delivered to Renfrew in March 1962 and served the Corporation until the last Herald service on 31 October 1966.

During 1962 BEA's Scottish services had been drastically reduced in frequency. On 1 April the three daily Glasgow-Aberdeen flights had been reduced to two and all other Scottish internal services had been cut to one a day. By the end of 1963 however the situation had improved sufficiently for a major competitor to appear on the Scottish trunk routes. This was British Eagle International Airlines, which had been re-acquired by Mr Harold Bamberg from the Cunard Group earlier that year. On 4 November 1963 British Eagle commenced services from London Airport to Glasgow and Edinburgh. Six round trips were operated each day, using former BOAC Britannias in direct competition with BEA's Vanguards. These aircraft were furnished with fourteen First Class and eighty-seven Tourist Class seats and the inaugural service to Renfrew was flown by aircraft G-AOVT. On 1 January 1964 British Eagle went on to take over Starways, who had been operating from Liverpool and Newquay to Glasgow since 1960. The Starways Dakotas used on these routes were promptly replaced by British Eagle Viscounts.

Despite the competition from British Eagle, or perhaps because of it, on 8 April 1964 BEA's London-Glasgow route became the first route on their network to carry half a million passengers in a twelve-month period.

At the beginning of May 1966 Abbotsinch was finally ready to take over the role of Glasgow's airport. The last scheduled service out of Renfrew was operated by a BEA Vanguard on the morning of 2 May 1966. The airport was then closed down and all airline operations were transferred to Abbotsinch on that day. During the period 1950-1965 the annual passenger traffic at Renfrew had grown from 131,789 to 1,276,623.

Glasgow's other airport at *Prestwick* was used principally for trans-Atlantic services and was the first airport in the United Kingdom to sell duty-free whiskey, a large purpose-built Duty Free Centre being opened there in November 1959 by millionaire Hugh Fraser. On 5 April 1951 a Comet 1 on a proving flight became the first jet airliner to visit Prestwick and in due course trans-Atlantic jet travel came to the airport. Over the years though there were also attempts at operating domestic routes out of Prestwick, and these met with varying degrees of success. The locally based Scottish Airlines ran a scheduled service throughout the 1950s from Prestwick to Northolt via Burtonwood Air Base, midway between Liverpool and Manchester. The thirty-six-seater Dakota G-AMPP was used for these flights and a fast car connection into London was provided, which Scottish Airlines claimed delivered their passengers to the English capital before BEA's direct Renfrew-London service which left Glasgow at the same time. Sometimes as many as three round trips a day were flown on this route, which continued in operation until 25 September 1960. By the end of 1958 G-AMPP was the only aircraft left in the Scottish Airlines fleet. Its last commercial service for them was from Belfast to Prestwick on 9 November 1960. The aircraft was then purchased by Dan-Air, along with the traffic rights for the Prestwick-Isle of Man route which Dan-Air continued to operate with the same Dakota.

In 1961 an ambitious attempt to mount a 'walk-on' shuttle-type service between Prestwick and London was made by Overseas Aviation (C.I.) Ltd. The route was the first scheduled service to be operated by Overseas, who were predominantly a holiday charter airline. A fleet of former Trans-Canada Air Lines Canadair North Stars were used on the route which incorporated a stop at Manchester in each direction. The first service departed Prestwick on 31 July 1961. Seat reservations were not necessary for the flights which operated on Mondays, Wednesdays and Fridays with one round trip on each day. Success was not forthcoming however and the service was terminated on 11 August 1961 after only twelve round trips had been completed and a little over 100 passengers carried.

BEA had commenced a Dakota service linking *Edinburgh* (Turnhouse) airport with Northolt in one direction and Aberdeen and Shetland in the other on 19 May 1947. This was to be interrupted later but an Aberdeen-Edinburgh-Northolt route was resumed in the spring of 1952 and on 26 October BEA introduced an Edinburgh-London weekly return fare of £8 for the duration of the winter. The winter of 1952/3 also saw the resumption of a through service from Aberdeen and Edinburgh to Manchester. The single fare between Edinburgh and Aberdeen was £3.5.0

(£3.25). Another destination was provided by BEA's Dakotas from 19 April 1953 when they inaugurated a Glasgow-Edinburgh-Birmingham-Northolt routing.

All of these routes were flown by Dakotas but back in 1950 Turnhouse airport had been the destination of the first-ever domestic air service to be operated by turbo-prop equipment. For the duration of the 1950 Edinburgh Festival BEA used the prototype Viscount G-AHRF for trial services between Northolt and Edinburgh. These lasted from 15-23 August 1950. Dakotas then resumed responsibility for the BEA schedules out of Edinburgh but from 1953 Viscount 700s began to take over the routes once more, this time on a permanent basis.

Other airlines operating into Turnhouse during the 1950s included Aer Lingus whose Dakota EI-ACE inaugurated their Dublin-Edinburgh service on 22 April 1952.

Another new operator was BKS Air Transport, with a Belfast-Edinburgh Dakota service in 1956. By the end of 1958 the route had been extended onwards to Newcastle but financial problems at BKS forced the suspension of the service in December 1961. The Belfast-Edinburgh link was eventually restored on 11 May 1964 when BKS flight BK642 was operated by their Ambassador aircraft G-ALZT.

In the meantime yet another new airline had come to Turnhouse with the opening of an Edinburgh-Isle of Man route by Silver City Airways on 1 June 1958. Heron and Bristol Wayfarer aircraft flew the schedules each Friday and Sunday. The Herons were disposed of at the end of the 1959 season but the service survived the absorbtion of Silver City into the British United Airways group, being operated thereafter by BUA(CI).

The most productive route out of Edinburgh continued to be the BEA service to London, which had been transferred to London Airport on the closure of Northolt. From December 1960 onwards BEA phased in their new and larger Vanguard turbo-props to cope with the increased loads but from November 1963 they were to face intense competition from British Eagle International Airlines. The British Eagle route licences from London to Edinburgh, Glasgow and Belfast were the first to be awarded to a British independent airline for services in direct competition with the state corporation. Ex-BOAC Britannia 312 turbo-props were used, with the inaugural flight of the daily service being flown by G-AOVT on 4 November 1963. British Eagle repeatedly applied for increases in the frequency of these flights and from 1 April 1964 ten trips each week were scheduled but this was still below the level the airline considered necessary for profitable operation. A further application for a frequency increase was rejected late in 1964 and as a consequence British Eagle withdrew the service as uneconomic on 20 February 1965.

A year or so later BEA once again had competition on the London route, this time from British United Airways out of Gatwick Airport. BUA operated a proving flight to Turnhouse for press representatives on 13 December 1965 and in January 1966 full BAC 1-11 'Interjet' services began.

BEA Viscount 701 G-AMOH sits outside the tiny terminal building on the east side of Dyce Airport, Aberdeen on 29 May 1956, during one of the first Viscount proving flights into the airport.

Aberdeen airport in the 1950s was nothing like the busy place it is today. Passengers bound for London had to change flights at Glasgow and the present-day terminal complex had not been built. In the BEA winter 1951/2 timetable only one service each day to Shetland and two to Orkney were listed. The standard equipment for these flights was the trusty Dakota and the combined daily passenger capacity of these northbound services was only thirty-five. The following winter BEA re-introduced their Aberdeen-Edinburgh service with an onward extension to Manchester. The single fares from Aberdeen at this time were: London £15.5.0 (£15.25), Edinburgh £3.5.0 (£3.25), Kirkwall (Orkney) £5.10.0 (£5.50) and Sumburgh (Shetland) £7.10.0 (£7.50). An eight-day excursion fare to London was also on offer for £11.5.0 (£11.25) return, a few shillings less than the First Class return rail fare. Flights were still operated by 'Pionair' class Dakotas to Edinburgh and then onward by connecting flight to Northolt.

The first Viscount to visit Aberdeen arrived on a proving flight in May 1956 and during that year the airport handled 28,385 terminating and 3,028 transit passengers. The traffic figures and the fares continued to climb and by January 1961 the single fare to London had increased to £22 and the excursion return fare to £14.18.0 (£14.90). On 1 November 1963 a direct Aberdeen-London service was finally inaugurated by BEA.

Across the border in *Newcastle* major developments in 1953 heralded the expansion of services throughout the next two decades. BKS Aero Charter opened their first ever scheduled service on 18 May 1953, from Greatham Airport, West Hartlepool, to Northolt. This service was to continue until 1956 and early in June 1953 BKS opened more new routes from both West Hartlepool and Woolsington Airport, Newcastle to the Isle of Man and Jersey. At the end of the year the company name was changed to BKS Air Transport, to reflect the change in emphasis from charter flights to scheduled service operations.

BKS Air Transport Ambassador G-ALZT undergoes maintenance at Woolsington Airport, Newcastle. BKS first introduced Ambassadors in August 1957, on the Newcastle-Dublin route.

Another major operator commenced scheduled services from Newcastle in 1953. This was Hunting Air Transport, who inaugurated a twice-daily Dakota service to Northolt on 15 May. The starting date had originally been set for 1 May but had to be postponed as the airport at Woolsington was not ready in time to accept Dakota aircraft. The fares on the Northolt service were set at £3.10.0 (£3.50) single and £7 return. More new Hunting services soon followed. On 23 May a daily summer service to Glasgow and thrice-weekly summer services to Paris and Basle via Luxembourg were opened. Two days later a thrice-weekly route to Amsterdam and Dusseldorf was inaugurated and in July Hunting Air Transport became the first independent airline to join the International Air Transport Association (IATA). In October 1953 Clan Line bought an interest in the airline and it was renamed Hunting-Clan Air Transport.

On 1 March 1954 Hunting-Clan changed their London terminal airport from Bovingdon to Northolt. This reduced the journey time into the city centre considerably, and to attract still more custom they laid on a special car service between Woolsington Airport and Sunderland Station. More international services were started in 1954, again using Dakota aircraft. On 9 April a route to Hamburg and Copenhagen was opened, along with a connecting flight from Manchester to Newcastle. Five days later Oslo and Stockholm were also linked to Newcastle. From 16 June the call at Stockholm was dropped and one at Stavanger substituted. Finally, on 1 December 1954, the airline began to use Vickers Vikings on the northern network in place of Dakotas, starting with the routes to Northolt, Stavanger and Oslo. At the height of the 1954 summer season Hunting-Clan were operating 35 flights each week out of Newcastle. The overall traffic figures for the airport in 1954 totalled 43,028 passengers and 4,310 aircraft movements.

During the winter of 1954/5 the airport facilities at Newcastle were upgraded. This work included the construction of a 5,500 feet paved runway to permit operations by the Viscount aircraft which Hunting-Clan were planning to introduce in the summer. In due course these operations came about with the inauguration of Viscount 700 services to Stavanger and Oslo. They were to prove uneconomical however and in August 1956 the northern route network of Hunting-Clan was taken over by Dragon Airways, who used Viking and Heron equipment until the end of the year when their operations too were suspended due to financial difficulties.

The other major operator at Newcastle was BKS Air Transport. They too were expanding and during the summer of 1956 they used Dakotas and Airspeed Consuls on a Woolsington-West Hartlepool-Leeds/Bradford-Bournemouth-Isle of Wight routing. Then on 1 April 1957 they inaugurated a Newcastle-Dublin Dakota operation. This service proved popular from the outset and over 2,000 seats had been sold before the first flight took off. On 9 August the Dakotas were superseded by Airspeed Ambassadors which BKS had purchased from BEA and converted to a fifty-five-seat high density layout. The following year the Ambassadors were used to open more new routes. A thrice-weekly schedule to Edinburgh and Belfast was commenced on 23 May 1958, followed by a fortnightly service to Bergen on 4 June. The most important new route though was inaugurated on 6 April 1960 when Ambassadors were used to renew the air link between Newcastle and London which had been dormant since Dragon Airways ceased operations in 1956. Three services each week were provided initially but this was soon increased.

Another new operator commenced scheduled services from Newcastle in April 1961 when Air Safaris opened their first scheduled route, linking the

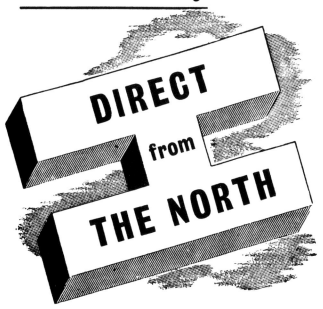

1953 advertisement for Hunting Air Transport's scheduled services from Newcastle Airport.

You can now fly

DIRECT from THE NORTH

To

PARIS · AMSTERDAM
DÜSSELDORF · LUXEMBOURG
BASLE

Also

Daily services between Glasgow & Newcastle
Twice daily between Newcastle & London

NEW LOW FARES

FREIGHT CARRIED ON ALL ROUTES

HUNTING

AIR TRANSPORT LTD.

A Hunting Group Company

Woolsington Airport, Newcastle upon Tyne 1. Tel: Newcastle 69051
5 Fitzhardinge Street, London, W.1. Tel: Welbeck 7799

HG 21

city with Birmingham and Bournemouth. Vickers Vikings were used but the service was destined not to last as Air Safaris ceased operating altogether on 31 October.

The BKS service to London continued to thrive and on 24 April 1964 Britannia 102 equipment took over from the Ambassadors. By then there were several services daily on the route. By 1965 the annual traffic total at Newcastle Airport had increased to 253,955 passengers aboard 18,184 aircraft movements.

The BKS Ambassadors which had served Newcastle so well were also used to open services from the new *Teesside* Airport (formerly RAF Middleton St George) on 20 August 1964. The first destination served was London and routes soon followed to Amsterdam and Dusseldorf, Belfast, Dublin, Jersey and Ostend.

Rapide G-AHKT of Yeadon Aviation Ltd in front of the old hangar at Yeadon Airport. The airline operated services from there until 1958.

Since May 1949 *Leeds/Bradford* Airport (or Yeadon as it was then known) had been linked to Northolt by the twice-daily Rapide and Consul services of the Lancashire Aircraft Corporation. This service was terminated on 2 February 1953 however when the Ministry of Civil Aviation who owned the airport withdrew their staff and facilities. All civil flying ceased until October 1953 when the resident operator Yeadon Aviation took over the running of the airport. In May 1955 they re-opened scheduled services with a summer-only Rapide operation to the Isle of Man. This service was reinstated for the 1956 and 1957 summer seasons and again in 1958 until Yeadon Aviation stopped operating in August of that year.

eturning holidaymakers disembark
om BKS Air Transport Dakota
-AMVC at Leeds/Bradford Airport
ter a flight from the Channel Islands
July 1961.

Meanwhile BKS Air Transport had also begun to use the airport and they were to go on to become the principal operator from Yeadon. In May 1955 they introduced a thrice-weekly Dakota service to Belfast and they followed this on 28 July with a route to Paris (Le Bourget). Other destinations served that year included Dusseldorf, the Isle of Wight, Jersey and Ostend.

At this time all international services had to be flown via Southend for customs clearance but on 1 May 1956 Yeadon received its own customs facilities and the calls at Southend were eliminated. During 1958 the main runway 10/28 was resurfaced and on 8 January 1959 the renamed Leeds/Bradford Airport was taken over by the Leeds and Bradford Joint Airport Committee. Runway and approach lighting was installed and the passenger terminal and apron were extended.

In 1959 BKS opened their own town terminal in Leeds and in July of that year they commenced services to Dublin with Dakotas. They had acquired Airspeed Ambassadors by this time but runway limitations prevented the operation of this more attractive aircraft from Leeds/Bradford. A new operator at the airport that year was North-South Airlines, who inaugurated a weekly schedule to Bournemouth on 6 June. This was a seasonal service using De Havilland Herons and these aircraft were also used on other summer-only routes to Exeter and Sandown (IOW) with an optional stop at Bournemouth. The flights were repeated during the next two summers but in January 1962 North-South relinquished their scheduled service licences and they were wound up in March.

The air link with London which had been broken in 1953 was restored on 3 October 1960 and it was BKS Air Transport who reopened the service, using London Airport instead of Northolt as before. Five Dakota round trips were operated each week initially but two years later the airline was finally able to place modern equipment onto the route in the shape of an Avro 748 turbo-prop on lease from Skyways Coach-Air. The first 748 service to London took place on 1 October 1962 and the leased machine was soon replaced by three of BKS's own examples. These new turbo-props offered greater capacity, with forty-four seats instead of thirty-six, and reduced the flying time to London by almost half an hour. During the next two years the 748s took over almost all the BKS services from Leeds/Bradford and were used to inaugurate routes to new destinations such as Amsterdam and Dusseldorf.

In October 1963 work started on a new 5,400 feet runway, which was completed in April 1965. This enabled larger aircraft to use the airport, including the BEA Viscount 800s which BKS leased on several occasions to cope with very heavy bookings on the London service.

Over the Pennines at *Carlisle* Airport an attempt was made in 1963 to operate a regular service to Gatwick. Derby Airways commenced a Dakota schedule on 1 April, but the service attracted no passengers at all during its first week of operation and only 20 during the second week, and so the service was withdrawn in May.

Much greater success was enjoyed further south at Squires Gate Airport, *Blackpool,* whose location directly opposite the Isle of Man made it ideal for short, low-cost crossings of the Irish Sea. During 1956 British Aviation Services, the parent company of Silver City Airways, bought out the Lancashire Aircraft Corporation and Manx Airlines, followed in February 1957 by Dragon Airways. These companies were amalgamated to form the northern division of Silver City Airways, based at Blackpool. From October 1957 the combined fleet of Herons and Bristol 170 Wayfarers wore Silver City markings whilst operating a network of routes including those from Blackpool to the Isle of Man and Jersey. In 1958 thirty-six seat Dakotas were added to the fleet and used to inaugurate new routes from Blackpool to Ostend and from Newcastle via Blackpool to the Isle of Man. Herons were used to open another new service, this time to Belfast. On 15 May 1959 a service to Dublin was opened in association with Aer Lingus and at the height of the

1959 season three Wayfarers, three Dakotas and two Herons were based at Blackpool. It was in a Wayfarer of Silver City that the author made his very first flight, from Blackpool to the Isle of Man in the summer of 1960.

Pegasus Airlines Viking 1B G-AJBT, ne of the aircraft used on their :heduled Blackpool-Gatwick service 1960–1961.

A new name appeared at Blackpool on 7 October 1960 when Pegasus Airlines opened a scheduled service to Gatwick. The flights were operated by Viking aircraft and took 1 hour 20 minutes. The service continued throughout the winter and the following summer until 25 October 1961 when Viking G-AHPL flew the final schedule to Gatwick on the day that Pegasus Airlines ceased trading. During their time on the route Pegasus had carried 5,064 passengers on 320 flights and had achieved an average load factor of almost forty-four per cent.

On 1 November 1962 the route networks of Silver City Airways and Jersey Airlines were merged to form British United (C.I.) Airways. Both of the constituent companies were already part of the Air Holdings Group, the parent company of British United Airways. Operations from Blackpool continued under the new identity and on 1 April 1963 a thrice-weekly service to Gatwick was opened using a thirty-two seat Dakota. The route was dropped on 30 September but was immediately taken over by Autair, who operated into Luton instead of Gatwick. Autair used thirty-six seat Vikings for their six round trips each week. During 1963-4 a fleet of Airspeed Ambassadors was acquired and these were occasionally substituted for the Vikings on the run to Luton. In 1964 Autair opened their own North London Air Terminal near Finchley Road tube station. Coaches were provided to convey passengers on the forty-minute journey from Luton.

On 1 January 1964 BUA (C.I.) commenced a twice-weekly Dakota service from Blackpool to Bournemouth via Manchester.

The local airline of the *Isle of Man* in the 1950s was Manx Airlines. Manx opened their first scheduled service in May 1950, using a single Rapide on flights to Carlisle. In 1953 two Dakotas were acquired and used on routes to Newcastle and Glasgow (Renfrew). The Rapide operation continued on a summer-only basis and Bristol 170 Wayfarers were introduced in May 1956. In 1957 the airline was bought out by British Aviation Services and amalgamated into the northern division of Silver City Airways, in whose colours the fleet then flew.

Speke Airport at *Liverpool* was the operating base for the world's first scheduled passenger service by helicopter, which was inaugurated by BEA on 1 June 1950. A Sikorsky S-51 helicopter was used for flights to Cardiff via an optional stop at Wrexham and the service continued until 31 March 1951, by which time 819 passengers had been carried. BEA also experimented that year with a Rapide service between Liverpool, Anglesey and Cardiff but the service was withdrawn after six months, during which period 603 passengers had been carried for a total revenue of £1,740, set against operating costs of £9,755.

Seen here at Blackpool (Squires Gate on 4 July 1962 is Bristol 170 Mk 2 G-AIFM, one of several used by Silver City on passenger services to the Isle of Man from 1957.

At that time BEA were the principal operator from Liverpool, but on 7 April 1951 Cambrian Air Services took over the route to Cardiff (Pengam Moors) under a BEA Associate Agreement. Cambrian also used Rapide aircraft on this, their first service from Liverpool. BEA operated Dakotas to Cardiff on Sundays during the summer season and on their Irish Sea routes. Aer Lingus were using Dakotas for their Dublin-Liverpool services, although Bristol 170 Wayfarers were occasionally substituted during the period 1952–1955.

In 1953 Cambrian acquired De Havilland Doves to replace the Rapides, and further expansion led to the introduction of Dakotas the following year.

A 'thumbs-up' from an engineer in the cockpit of a BEA Dakota at Liverpool in the early 1950s.

Also in 1953, Newcastle-based Dragon Airways took over the assets of Liverpool operator Wright Aviation. Among the directors of Dragon Airways was Mr Harold Bamberg, the founder of Eagle Aviation who were later to become a major scheduled operator from Liverpool under the name of British Eagle International Airlines. Dragon Airways based a Rapide aircraft at Liverpool in 1953 and used this principally for charter work but it was also flown on a scheduled service to Glasgow until the route was upgraded to Heron equipment on 28 June 1955.

Another new Liverpool operator at this time was Starways Ltd., who inaugurated a scheduled service to London in March 1955. The service operated thrice-weekly, initially using thirty-six seat Dakotas.

On 9 May 1955 BEA and Cambrian signed a ten-year agreement covering services between the Channel Islands and mainland Britain under which BEA's Liverpool-Channel Isles route was transferred to Cambrian. Cambrian added Herons to their fleet in 1956 and for that summer only Dragon Airways operated a Newcastle-Liverpool-Paris Viking service.

BEA reduced their shareholding in Aer Lingus to ten per cent in 1957 and were granted traffic rights to Dublin for the first time in April. From then onwards they operated Liverpool-Dublin schedules in competition with Aer Lingus.

During 1958 Starways increased the frequency of their Liverpool-London service to one each weekday plus additional flights on Tuesday, Wednesday and Thursday, thus providing a day-return facility on those days. When passenger loads were heavy a seventy-two seater DC-4 was used in place of the usual Dakota. On 15 December Aer Lingus introduced F-27 Friendships on their Liverpool-Dublin flights, but the year did not prove so successful for Cambrian Airways, who sustained severe losses and put their entire fleet up for sale at the end of the summer season. The airline was saved from liquidation by the intervention of BEA who had purchased a shareholding earlier in the year, and services resumed in 1959 using leased BEA Dakotas.

An apron scene at Liverpool in the early 1960s. Behind the Starways Dakota are Viscounts of Starways and BEA.

Starways however continued to prosper and to extend their route network from Liverpool. During 1959 they opened a DC-4 service to Newquay and in October 1960 they inaugurated a Liverpool-Glasgow service with Dakota aircraft. Two round trips were operated each Tuesday, Wednesday and Thursday.

New turbo-prop equipment for Starways arrived at Liverpool on 3 February 1961 when their first Viscount 700 was delivered. After a period of route proving and crew training the Viscount entered service on 10 June, but Starways were not the first Viscount operator at the airport as BEA had introduced the type on their Irish Sea routes in place of Dakotas on 1 April 1960.

On 4 April 1960 Dan-Air inaugurated their first domestic scheduled service. This was from Bristol and Cardiff to Liverpool. Eight-seater Dove aircraft were used and on 16 July the route was extended southwards to Plymouth. From 4 January 1961 the route continued onwards from Liverpool to Newcastle and in July the Doves were superseded by Dakotas. Dakotas were also used to open a Liverpool-Rotterdam service on 9 January 1962. From 1965 Airspeed Ambassadors were used in place of Dakotas and the Dutch destination was changed to Amsterdam.

Cambrian Airways took over all the BEA Irish Sea services to Dublin, Belfast and the Isle of Man on 1 April 1963 and operated them with a fleet of former BEA Viscount 701s. From October the flights to Belfast used the new airport at Aldergrove which had been officially opened by HM The Queen Mother on 28 October 1963, and which replaced Nutts Corner Airport.

During 1963 some of the Starways flights to London began to incorporate a call at Hawarden Airport, Chester but on 1 January 1964 Starways were taken over by British Eagle International Airlines. British Eagle established an engineering base at Liverpool and increased the frequency of the London route to three daily services. Britannia aircraft operated the first flight of the day and Viscounts flew the other two, one of which called at Hawarden. The Glasgow route was also upgraded to a twice-daily Viscount operation. Cambrian also began operating to London from 20 January, as part of a daily Viscount flight which originated in the Isle of Man.

During the summer of 1964 British Eagle's scheduled service network included fifteen routes out of six provincial cities in addition to the services out of London. In 1965 the airline introduced further new routes from Liverpool, to Rimini via Manchester and to Palma via Birmingham, and increased the number of London flights to thirty-nine each week.

SABENA Caravelle OO-SRC arrived at Liverpool on a football supporters' charter from Brussels on 26 November 1964 and became the first pure-jet airliner to land at the airport.

On 7 February 1949 a new passenger terminal was opened in former wartime buildings at *Manchester* (Ringway) Airport. BEA introduced a Glasgow-Manchester-Paris Dakota service on 16 April and followed this in the following month with a summer route to Jersey via Birmingham. From 22 May this was upgraded to a daily frequency.

Another summer-only destination was served from Manchester in 1950 by Finglands Aviation, who inaugurated a service to Newquay on 5 August. Avro Anson Is flew two trips each Saturday at a fare of £9.16.0 (£9.80) return. The route was reinstated for the 1951 and 1952 seasons but Finglands ceased all flying operations in September 1952 and the Ansons were disposed of.

A milestone in the development of Ringway occurred in late January 1951 when a new approach radar unit was commissioned. Further improvements followed, including the extension of the main runway from 4,200 feet to 5,900 feet, which was completed on 6 November 1951, and the introduction of twenty-four hour operation on 1 April 1952. Night mail services were operated to Belfast by BEA and to Dublin by Aer Lingus from 12 March

The enquiry desk in the interim terminal at Manchester Airport on 6 April 1961. An impressive list of destinations is displayed.

1951, using Dakotas on the first regular all-mail services between the United Kingdom and Ireland. The increase in runway length persuaded BEA to begin using Vikings on some passenger routes in place of Dakotas. One of the first Viking-operated services was the air link to London which had not been flown for the past four years. The new service was inaugurated on 2 April 1952, on which date a Viking schedule to Zurich was also introduced. Other destinations to receive Viking services that year included Belfast, Amsterdam and Dusseldorf.

During a twelve-week period from 28 June 1952 Air France operated a Saturday flight from Dinard to Manchester with Douglas DC-4s. At that time these were the largest aircraft operating scheduled services into Manchester.

Agreement was reached on 3 November 1952 that Manchester Corporation should retain control of Ringway Airport and it was to remain municipally owned throughout the period covered by this book. During 1952 163,000 passengers passed through the airport.

The first visit of a turbine-powered airliner to Manchester (Ringway). BEA V.701 Viscount G-ALWE is fuelled by a vintage Shell bowser outside the interim terminal building on 20 March 1953, prior to giving demonstration flights to local travel agents.

The first turbine-powered airliner to land at Ringway arrived on 20 March 1953 when BEA Viscount 701 G-ALWE flew in on a route-proving and demonstration flight, but it was to be over a year before the type began commercial operations from Manchester. In the meantime BEA introduced their 'Elizabethan' class Airspeed Ambassadors in place of Vikings on many routes, including the services to London on 17 May 1953 and the schedules to Paris via Birmingham and to Dusseldorf via Amsterdam on 5 and 6 October respectively.

Other aircraft types new to Manchester that year included the Convair 240s of SABENA on their Brussels-Manchester route. OO-AWO operated the inaugural Convair service on 21 April 1953 in a forty-seat configuration. SABENA had been flying the route with Dakotas since 1949 and from April 1957 the larger Convair 340s and 440s were phased in. DC-4s were also used by SABENA on a Brussels-Ostend-Manchester routing from 13 June 1953. On a slightly smaller scale, Jersey Airlines replaced Rapides with De Havilland Herons on their Jersey-Manchester schedules from 6 June and during that summer local operator Airviews Ltd. operated a seasonal Rapide service to Southampton and the Isle of Wight.

1954 was the year that Viscounts took over on many routes from Manchester. On 11 April BEA introduced them on their services to London and to Paris via Birmingham, followed by the Amsterdam and Dusseldorf route two days later. They were also used on a weekend service to Zurich. On 29 September one of the passengers on a BEA 'Pionair' Dakota service to the Isle of Man became the millionth post-war passenger to pass through Ringway.

Passengers from Amsterdam disembark from KLM Convair 240 PH-TEH and enter the interim terminal at Ringway Airport, Manchester in 1953.

SABENA Convair 240 OO-AWP is
fuelled at Manchester after a flight
from Brussels in 1953.

In January 1955 Jersey Airlines made a proving flight from Manchester to
Dinard, carrying the Lord Mayor of Manchester and representatives of the
press aboard a Heron aircraft. Full scheduled services on the route began in
June. Other new services inaugurated that year included a BEA night
Viscount schedule to Milan and Eagle Airways services to Munich and
Vienna using thirty-six seat 'Mayfair' class Vikings. Hunting-Clan Air
Transport opened their 'Africargo' freight service to East Africa via London
on 23 July, initially using Avro Yorks.

On 23 September 1955 the name of the airport was officially changed from
Ringway to Manchester Airport.

Despite their gradual displacement from the BEA route network Dakotas
were still used to inaugurate a new route on 29 October 1956. The operator
was not BEA though, but Cambrian Airways and the destination was the
Channel Islands via intermediate stops at Cardiff and Bristol.

Other airlines introducing Viscounts onto their schedules in 1957 included
KLM, who were to continue to use srs 800s on their Amsterdam-Manchester
route until 1967. Aer Lingus began Viscount flights from Dublin to
Manchester and onwards to Amsterdam on 14 April and the next day another
new routing from Dublin to Brussels and Frankfurt via Manchester was
inaugurated. Yet another new service, from Dublin to Manchester and on to
Zurich and Rome was opened by Aer Lingus Viscounts on 27 June. Eagle

Airways also used Viscounts alongside Vikings on a thrice-weekly schedule to Hamburg and Copenhagen which was introduced on 3 June.

SABENA used Convair 440s on summer weekend flights to Ostend and Airviews operated De Havilland Doves on services to Newcastle (twice-weekly) and Newquay (three times weekly) during the year.

In order to keep pace with this continual traffic growth work commenced on the foundations of a new terminal building in October 1957 and a further extension of the main runway to 7,000 feet was declared operational on 23 April 1958.

A preview of future airline equipment was provided when a Caravelle demonstration aircraft became the first pure-jet airliner to visit Manchester Airport, landing there on 30 July 1958. Another new type that year was the Fokker F-27 Friendship turbo-prop, which Aer Lingus placed onto their service from Dublin and continued to operate into Manchester until 1966.

The Aer Lingus Viscount service to Dusseldorf was extended onwards to Copenhagen on 4 April 1959 and on the following day Austrian Airlines began operating Viscounts into Manchester from Vienna and Frankfurt. Also during the year Eagle Airways used their rather elderly Vikings on fortnightly schedules to Ostend and to Bergen.

The former Airviews service to Newquay was re-opened on 19 June 1960 by Starways, who also included a stop at Exeter.

The first European jet schedule to Manchester was inaugurated by Air France on 1 June 1961 when Caravelle F-BHRD arrived from Paris. A summer-only service to the Isle of Wight was provided by Mercury Airlines in 1961 and was reinstated for the 1962 season along with another new route to Exeter. Another summer service in 1962 was opened by Eagle Airways, flying DC-6As to Bergen via Newcastle.

The new terminal at Manchester Airport was officially opened on 22 October 1962 and came into full use on 3 December. The new building incorporated two passenger piers and a tower block containing offices and air traffic control services.

From 1 November 1963 BEA introduced low stand-by fares on their London-Manchester flights.

Mercury Airlines introduced a five-times weekly service to Teesside Airport in 1964 but the company ceased operations in October. SABENA replaced the Convair 440s on their Brussels service with Caravelle jets from 1 April 1964, and more jet services came along the following year with the first BAC 1-11 service from Manchester, to Frankfurt by Aer Lingus on 7 June 1965, and the introduction of Trident 1s on BEA's Paris route on 1 July in response to the challenge from Air France's Caravelles.

Regional Scheduled Services — South

One of the major operators in the Midlands during the early 1950s was Don Everall (Aviation) Ltd. From 1953 onwards they flew services to the Channel Islands and the Isle of Man from *Birmingham* (Elmdon) and from Coventry, Leicester and Wolverhampton airports. Rapide equipment was used initially and in May 1955 these aircraft opened a Birmingham-Sandown (IOW) route which had to be suspended at the end of the 1956 summer season because of the poor condition of the grass airfield at Sandown. In April 1957 the company acquired their first Dakota which was placed into service on the scheduled routes. By 1960 however all the services to the Isle of Man had been terminated and the only routes still in operation were those from Birmingham and Coventry to the Channel Isles. In November 1960 Don Everall Aviation merged with Air Safaris Ltd., and the following season's schedules were flown by aircraft wearing Air Safaris colours. The route network for the summer of 1961 included services from Birmingham to Exeter, Guernsey, Jersey and the Isle of Wight and a new route from Newcastle to Birmingham and Bournemouth which was inaugurated on 3 June. By the end of the season though Air Safaris were in financial trouble and they ceased operations on 31 October 1961.

In the meantime BEA had also been active at Birmingham. Dakota services to Belfast (Nutts Corner) Airport had commenced on 1 May 1950 and on 13 May a summer-only Manchester-Birmingham-Jersey Dakota routing was opened. Vikings were introduced on 19 April 1953 on a new service which came South from Glasgow and Edinburgh and continued onwards to Northolt, and more new equipment came to Elmdon on 5 October when BEA's 'Elizabethan' class Airspeed Ambassadors began operating on their Manchester-Birmingham-Paris route. The 'Elizabethans' were themselves superseded by Viscount turbo-props on the schedules to Manchester and Paris and on daily Birmingham-London services from 11 May 1954.

Birmingham was also involved in BEA's experiments with helicopter passenger operations. On 1 June 1951 an experimental service was launched between London Airport, Northolt Airport and Birmingham (Haymills Rotorstation). The 'King Arthur' class Sikorsky S-51s used could carry a pilot and three passengers at a cruising speed of 90 mph. On the first flights invited guests only were carried but from 4 June the service was opened to the public at a single fare of £2.10.0 (£2.50). The route was flown thrice-daily except Sundays but on 9 April 1952 the passenger facility was withdrawn and the service became cargo-only. In 1953 the S-51s were replaced by BEA's new Bristol 171 helicopters but the operation was suspended on 14 January 1954. This was not the end of BEA helicopter trials in the area altogether, for on 2 July 1956 another experimental service was opened between Birmingham, Leicester and Nottingham. Sikorsky S-55s were used on two flights each weekday and by the end of the trial period on 10 November 1956, 1,829 passengers had been carried.

On 23 April 1956 Birmingham was incorporated as a stop on BEA's Manchester-Dusseldorf Viscount route, and this type of aircraft was to become the mainstay of the airline's services out of Birmingham for many years to come. Aer Lingus also used Viscounts to replace Dakotas on their schedules from Dublin and the type was still being used to open new routes in 1965 when British Eagle inaugurated a Liverpool-Birmingham-Palma service.

Derby Aviation became a scheduled service operator on 18 July 1953 with a summer service from DERBY (Burnaston) to Jersey via Wolverhampton. An eight-seater Rapide aircraft was used and the route was reinstated for the following summer, along with new services from Birmingham and Nottingham to the Channel Isles. By the summer of 1954 a fleet of four Rapides was in service. The airline's first Dakota was delivered in April 1955 and operated in a thirty-six-seat configuration. Also acquired that year were two Miles Marathon feeder-liners which were furnished as either eighteen or twenty-seaters. Derby Aviation were destined to be the only commercial operator of this type in Britain. The Marathons were not equipped with de-icing apparatus and so were only used in the summer months, on schedules to Jersey and on the airline's first international route, from Derby to Ostend that year. These aircraft were also used to inaugurate more new routes from Derby to Glasgow and the Isle of Man that summer. At the end of the 1956 season the routes from Wolverhampton were dropped altogether but in 1958 the Marathons were utilised on newly-opened schedules to the Channel Islands from two new departure points, Northampton and Oxford. The short-field performance of the Marathons made them ideal for operations from these grass airfields. The following year yet another new route to the Channel Isles, this time from *Gloucester/Cheltenham* (Staverton) Airport, was pioneered by the Marathons but at the end of the 1960 season the type was withdrawn from use.

Miles Marathon G-AMHR *Monsaldale* of Derby Airways. Three Marathons were used for service from grass airfields such as Derby (Burnaston) in the late 1950s.

By 1959 however the Dakota fleet had grown to five aircraft and a total of eighteen destinations were being served. In 1959 the company was renamed Derby Airways Ltd., and in that year customs facilities were granted to Burnaston, thus eliminating the need for en route stops for clearance on international flights.

On 1 October 1964 the airline was again re-named and became British Midland Airways. The first turbo-prop aircraft was a Handley Page Herald which was delivered to Burnaston in February 1965 for use on domestic routes. By then the grass airfield at Burnaston was proving unsuitable for the larger types of aircraft in service or in prospect and work was well under way on a new airport at nearby Castle Donington. This was opened in April 1965 as the East Midlands Airport, and with its opening British Midland transferred all their operations there.

Over the border in Wales Cambrian Air Services used Rapide aircraft to re-open the route from *Cardiff* to Liverpool which BEA had previously operated. Cambrian inaugurated their service on 7 April 1951, flying out of Pengam Moors Airport at Cardiff under a BEA Associate Agreement.

An apron scene at Cardiff (Rhoose) Airport in August 1956, featuring Heron G-AORJ and Dakota G-AMSX of resident operator Cambrian Airways.

Shortly after this Aer Lingus commenced thrice-weekly Dakota schedules into *Bristol* (Whitchurch) Airport. The first service was on 3 May 1951 and Aer Lingus followed this the next summer with an inaugural flight into Cardiff on 13 June 1952. As Aer Lingus were using the larger Dakota aircraft their Cardiff flights were operated into Rhoose Airport. During the winter of 1952/3 their Cardiff and Bristol schedules were combined.

Cambrian opened a feeder route from *Haverfordwest* to Cardiff on 24 May 1952. Rapides were used for the forty-five minute journey to Pengam Moors, where connections were available to Liverpool, Weston-Super-Mare and the Channel Islands.

1953 was a year of expansion for Cambrian. In February they purchased part of the Olley Air Service fleet of Doves, and under an agreement with Morton Air Services they took over the routes from Bristol to Guernsey and Jersey on 1 April. They also bought out Staverton-based Murray Chown Aviation in 1953 and took over their route from Staverton to the Channel Isles. This summer-only service was flown via Bournemouth for customs clearance. That same year Cambrian opened a new Cardiff-Bristol-Paris service, using Dove aircraft from 24 May and another summer service from Cardiff to Dinard. During the year over 18,000 passengers were carried at an average load factor of almost eighty per cent.

The introduction of aircraft larger than the Rapides which were then being phased out meant that the 2,900 feet runway at Pengam Moors was no longer suitable for Cambrian's operations at Cardiff, and in 1954 they followed Aer Lingus in moving to Rhoose Airport. The airline name was changed to Cambrian Airways on 23 May 1955 to reflect the new accent on scheduled services and to coincide with the introduction of Dakotas, one of which was used on 20 June to inaugurate their longest route to date, a weekly service from Cardiff to Nice. The following year another new destination came on-line from Cardiff when one of Cambrian's newly-acquired Heron aircraft opened a thrice-weekly schedule to Belfast via Bristol on 7 May 1956.

The official opening of Fairwood Common Airport at *Swansea* took place on 1 June 1957 and on that date Cambrian began a thrice-weekly Heron service from Swansea to Jersey. The routes out of Staverton however were dropped that year.

At the end of the 1958 season Cambrian were obliged to suspend all operations and put their entire aircraft fleet up for sale, but services resumed in 1959 using Dakotas leased from BEA. In 1960 the leased Dakotas were bought outright.

More scheduled services came to Bristol in 1960 when Dan-Air were invited by the local council to open the first routes out of the new airport at Lulsgate. Dan-Air inaugurated a thrice-weekly schedule from Bristol and Cardiff to Liverpool on 4 April 1960 using eight-seater Dove aircraft on what was the airline's first mainland domestic scheduled service. On 16 July the route was extended southwards to Plymouth and from 4 January 1961 it continued onwards from Liverpool to Newcastle. Dakotas took over from the Doves in July 1961.

Cardiff was the departure point for Dan-Air's first international schedule, which was a seasonal route to Basle via Bristol and was inaugurated with Dakota equipment on 16 July 1960.

Cambrian Airways became the first British airline to operate into the newly-opened Cork Airport when they commenced Dakota services from Bristol and Cardiff on 16 October 1961, and a direct link between the South-West and the North of England and Scotland was forged on 29 April 1962 with a new Dakota service from Bristol and Cardiff to Manchester and Glasgow.

Turbo-prop speed and comfort came to Cambrian's scheduled service network on 20 February 1963 with the inaugural Viscount service from Cardiff and Bristol to Dublin. A substantial number of ex-BEA Viscount 701s were acquired in the following years and these aircraft were to replace the Dakotas as the workhorse of the Cambrian fleet.

Down at the south-western tip of Britain BEA were operating services to the *Scilly Isles* in 1950, carrying tourists, residents and supplies from St Just Airport, Lands End to St Mary's in 'Islander' class Rapide biplanes. Three aircraft were used on the run during the busy summer months but in winter a single machine maintained the service. The twenty-minute flight compared favourably with an unpredictable three-hour sea crossing and some 20,000 passengers were carried annually in the Rapides. For many years they were the only aircraft licenced to fly commercially into the tiny airfield at St Mary's. They were finally replaced on 2 May 1964 by Sikorsky S-61 helicopters operated by BEA Helicopters Ltd. from Penzance Heliport on what was Europe's first scheduled service by multi-engined helicopters.

BEA 'Islander' class Rapide used on eir Channel Islands routes and on the nd's End-Scilly Isles run.

The first aircraft operated by British Westpoint was Dakota G-ALYF *Sir France Drake,* seen here undergoing maintenance at Exeter.

The Scillies were also served by Mayflower Air Services who commenced their first scheduled service from Plymouth to St Mary's on 26 February 1962. A single Rapide was used on this summer-only service and the following year Mayflower opened two more routes from the mainland. A flight to Exeter was timed to connect with the Mercury Airlines service from Manchester and a similar connection was provided at Newquay with Starways flights from Glasgow, Liverpool and Newcastle. To operate these additional schedules and also another new route from Cardiff to the Scillies, a second Rapide was acquired in 1963. The loss of one of these aircraft in a take-off crash brought about grave financial problems for the airline and in May 1964 it was taken over by British Westpoint Airlines. Mayflower continued to operate under its own name for the 1964 season and in conjunction with British Westpoint was able to offer connections through to London but by the end of the summer the two airlines' operations had been fully integrated under the British Westpoint name.

British Westpoint had commenced operations as Westpoint Aviation in March 1961. A single Dakota was used initially for charter work from their *Exeter* base but in 1963 the company name was changed and the first scheduled service was inaugurated on 1 April. This was a weekday operation from Newquay and Exeter to London Airport. An acquaintance of the author's remembers travelling aboard a British Westpoint Dakota from London to Exeter that year. Passengers were instructed to assemble at the 'General Haig' public house in Hounslow, from where they were collected by a minibus driven by a gentleman in white overalls. After landing at Exeter they discovered that the 'gentleman in white overalls' had just flown them there and was also the captain of the aircraft! After absorbing Mayflower Air Services in 1964 the company purchased BEA's last three Rapides. The 1965 season was not financially successful however and the Exeter-London service was only operated sporadically. After a poor winter's trading the airline ceased flying and went into liquidation in May 1966. International services were also available from Exeter by Jersey Airlines, who inaugurated a Dakota schedule to Dublin on 24 June 1960.

British Westpoint Airlines Rapide G-AJCL runs up its engines at their Exeter Airport base in 1964/5. Note the period cars in the background.

Another centre of airline activity in the West Country was *Newquay* Airport. In 1959 Starways opened a DC-4 service from Liverpool and during the following summer they also operated to Newquay from Birmingham, Manchester, Leeds/Bradford, Glasgow, London and Newcastle.

A direct air service from London to the Scilly Isles was launched in 1963 by Scillonian Air Services. Modern six-seater Aero Commander 500 executive aircraft were used for the flights from Gatwick Airport. The initial timetable provided for services on Mondays, Wednesdays and Saturdays, and the inaugural flight left Gatwick on 14 September 1963. The route licence also permitted an optional stop at Lands End and from 1 October the frequency was reduced to twice-weekly. By the end of the year fifty-eight sectors had been flown and ninety-five passengers carried, an average of two to three on each complete service. The operation was suspended for the winter months but was re-introduced on a daily basis for the following summer. Extra legs were flown when loads demanded but after the last flight of the season on 10 October 1964 the company's route licences were revoked and Scillonian ceased operations.

Hurn Airport at *Bournemouth* was used continually throughout the 1950s and 1960s as a convenient departure point for short flights to the Channel Islands, but various attempts were also made to link the airport with other mainland points. North-South Airlines inaugurated a scheduled service to Leeds/Bradford on 6 June 1959 using Heron equipment. The weekly flights continued until the end of September 1961 but they were not resumed the following year as North-South Airlines was wound up in March 1962. In April 1961 Air Safaris commenced services to Amsterdam via Ostend on a twice-weekly basis and from Bournemouth to Dublin. Another new route from Newcastle and Birmingham to Bournemouth, was opened on 3 June 1961. All these services were flown by Viking aircraft but Air Safaris ceased trading shortly after their last service from Bournemouth to Dublin on 27 October 1961. On 1 January 1964 British United Airways began operating a twice-weekly Dakota service from Bournemouth to Manchester and Blackpool.

Along the South Coast at *Southampton* (Eastleigh) Airport, Heron services to Paris were opened by Cambrian Air Services in 1953. Connections were available at Southampton from Bristol, Cardiff and Staverton. Southampton was also used for one of BEA's experimental helicopter services during 1954. Bristol 171 helicopters were operated from London Airport via Northolt to Southampton, with the official opening of the route taking place on 15 June 1954. On the following day seats went on sale to the public at fares of 30/- (£1.50) single and 50/- (£2.50) return. From 22 December a variation of this service was introduced which originated at Gatwick and flew to Southampton via London Airport, using Sikorsky S-55 helicopters in place of the Bristol 171s. BEA had commenced fixed-wing operations from Southampton in 1950, using Rapides to Alderney, Guernsey and Jersey. These aircraft were replaced by Dakotas on the route to Jersey, but when the Dakotas were in turn superseded by Viscounts the grass runway at Eastleigh was no longer suitable and the departure point was transferred to Bournemouth. BEA eventually returned to Southampton in April 1966 after a new concrete runway was opened, but the first scheduled flight to use the new runway was in fact a British United Airways Dakota which landed from Jersey on 25 September 1965.

The *Channel Islands* had their own local airline in the form of Jersey Airlines, which had been founded in 1948. The first commercial flight was a charter from Jersey to St Brieuc on 9 March 1949 with a leased Rapide aircraft and by the summer of 1950 the airline had five Rapides in service. Jersey Airlines operated their first scheduled services the following summer, from Jersey and Guernsey to Southampton. In 1952 more new routes connected Jersey with Exeter, Plymouth, Bournemouth, Gatwick, Manchester and Coventry. All these services utilised Rapide aircraft, which BEA also operated as the 'Islander' class on their own Channel Island schedules.

On 5 May 1953 Jersey Airlines became the first British airline to operate the De Havilland Heron. Heron 1 G-AMYU inaugurated their new Jersey-Paris route on that day and the fifteen-seater aircraft also entered service on the route to Gatwick four days later. By the summer of 1954 three Herons were in service and they had taken over much of the airline's route network. It was a Heron that opened a new weekend schedule to Bilbao on 11 May 1955 and this service was to continue in operation until 1961.

On 9 March 1956 BEA withdrew their remaining Rapides from the Channel Isles routes and at the end of that month they entered into an operating agreement with Jersey Airlines. BEA handed over all their Alderney services to Jersey Airlines and suspended their Southampton-Guernsey schedules. In return Jersey Airlines terminated their Jersey-Southampton service. When Gatwick Airport closed for reconstruction in 1956 Jersey Airlines transferred their London terminus to Croydon until the re-opening of Gatwick in 1958. After the official opening ceremony on 9 June 1958 a Jersey Airlines Heron operated the first scheduled departure from the new facilities, a flight to Alderney.

During 1956 more operators had begun to serve the Channel Isles. On 1 June 1956 Dan-Air used Jersey as the destination for their first ever scheduled service, a summer-only Dakota operation from Blackbushe. This was operated each summer from Blackbushe until the closure of that airport in May 1960 caused the transfer of the London terminus to Gatwick Airport. Cambrian Airways also used Dakotas to open a Manchester-Bristol-Cardiff-Channel Isles service on 29 October 1956. Jersey Airlines began operating their own Dakotas on 2 May 1959. The first destination to receive Dakota service was Bournemouth and the Dakotas were soon found to be suitable for operation into all the airports on the Jersey Airlines route network except for Alderney and Plymouth which continued to be served by Rapides for the time being.

BEA became the first Viscount operator to the Channel Islands when they introduced Viscount 700s, but Jersey Airlines were also planning to purchase modern turbo-prop aircraft and in September 1960 they became the first airline in the world to place an order for Handley Page Heralds. Four examples were purchased at a total cost of £1½ million and pending their delivery the demonstrator aircraft G-APWA was leased and placed into service on the Bournemouth route on 16 May 1961. During that year the last of the Rapides was disposed of.

Channel Airways operated Rapide G-AEMH from 1952 until 1961. It is seen here at Shoreham Airport on the afternoon of 28 August 1954. The magazine advertised is, alas, no longer with us.

In 1962 the airline's longest domestic route was opened from Jersey to Glasgow (Renfrew) but on 1 November Jersey Airlines was merged with the northern division of Silver City Airways to form British United (C.I.) Airways. Both companies had previously been acquired by the Air Holdings Group and were already part of the British United Airways group of companies. Because of the high esteem in which it was held by the travelling public Jersey Airlines was allowed to continue flying under its own name until the end of the 1963 summer season.

In 1950 Island Air Services operated a series of charter flights from SHOREHAM Airport to Deauville on behalf of casino owners in the Deauville area. Rapide aircraft were used to carry British gamblers who wished to try their luck at the tables in Deauville. These flights later attained scheduled service status when a BEA Associate Agreement was granted and IATA-agreed fares were introduced. The airline's Managing Director was Monique Agazarian, who commanded some of the flights and thereby gained the distinction of becoming the first woman ever to command an airliner on an international scheduled service. The lure of the casinos attracted many television and stage personalities onto the Island Air Services flights. The other major user of Shoreham Airport at this time was East Anglian Flying Services (later to be renamed Channel Airways) who operated feeder flights to Southend to connect with their cross-Channel services from 1953 until 1962.

Routes from *Southend* to Ostend and Jersey were introduced in 1949 and 1950 by East Anglian Flying Services but the airline ran into financial difficulties and had to suspend these services in 1951. The flights were re-activated in 1952 using Rapide aircraft. On 1 April 1954 East Anglian re-opened IPSWICH Airport, which it had leased from Ipswich Corporation, and opened feeder services to connect with the mainline routes. During 1954 the airline employed thirty staff in all and carried just over 6,500 passengers. The new Rotterdam Airport opened for business on 1 October 1956 and on this date Channel Airways (as East Anglian Flying Services was now called) commenced their first year-round scheduled service, a twice-daily operation from Southend to Rotterdam. De Havilland Dove aircraft were used on the route and a special introductory fare of nine guineas (£9.45) return was offered for the winter months. In 1957 the airline acquired two Bristol 170s for use on projected car-ferry services. These never materialised but the aircraft were retained and used in an all-passenger configuration. More new aircraft types followed, Vickers Vikings being introduced in 1958 and Dakotas in 1960. For high-density traffic on the short cross-Channel routes a Douglas DC-4 was purchased and converted by Field Aircraft Services to carry a record eighty-eight passengers, the aircraft entering service on 11 May 1963. Channel Airways took over another Southend-based airline, Tradair, on 31 December 1962 and inherited more Vikings plus two Viscount 700s, their first turbo-prop airliners. Several more Viscounts were purchased from BEA at the end of 1963 and the Viking fleet was then retired.

On 14 June 1952 Airwork and Hunting Air Transport opened their joint 'Safari' service to Nairobi. The Airwork flights departed from Blackbushe, where Viking G-AJFS was photographed in the mid-1950s.

Chapter 8

Colonial Coach Services

At the beginning of the 1950s Britain still had many colonial possessions throughout Africa and because air travel from Britain to these 'cabotage' points was exempt from the normal regulations governing international air fares the Colonial Coach class services were introduced by the independent UK airlines as a low-cost alternative to BOAC's flights. The fares on offer were considerably lower than those charged by BOAC but in return passengers had to accept travel in older and slower aircraft such as the Vickers Vikings, which needed to make at least one night-stop en route to the final destination. Despite this drawback the services were eagerly received and well patronised until the granting of independence to the remaining colonies and the introduction of new low excursion fares by BOAC and the local national carriers at the beginning of the 1960s brought about their withdrawal.

The first Colonial Coach service was the 'Safari' service to Nairobi which was operated jointly by Airwork Ltd. and Hunting Air Transport. The inaugural schedule departed on 14 June 1952 and arrived in Nairobi two days later. Stops were made at Nice, Malta (nightstop), El Adem, Wadi Halfa, Khartoum (nightstop), Juba and Entebbe. Two nightstops were also made on the return leg. A weekly frequency was provided, with alternating flights by Airwork Vikings from Blackbushe Airport near Camberley and by Hunting Vikings from Bovingdon Airport in Hertfordshire. Within the first nine months the load factor had reached ninety-three per cent without diverting traffic from BOAC's flights and by 1954 the frequency had been increased to twice weekly.

On 3 April 1953 Central African Airways had opened their own Colonial Coach operation, the weekly 'Zambesi' service from Salisbury to London. Vikings were also used for this operation. A reciprocal service from London was inaugurated by Airwork and Hunting Air Transport on 26 June, again using the faithful Vikings. Hunting flew the first schedule and thereafter each airline contributed one flight each month, thus providing a fortnightly schedule. The outbound routing was via Nice, Malta, Mersa Matruh, Wadi Halfa, Khartoum, Juba, Entebbe, Tabora, Ndola and Lusaka. The fare to Salisbury was £115 single and £207 return, that to Lusaka was £112.10.0 (£112.50) single or £202.10.0 (£202.50) return and a ticket to Ndola cost £111 single or £199.16.0 (£119.80) return. These fares included all meals and hotel accommodation en route, the tickets were interchangeable between the two airlines and the free baggage allowance was 44lb (20kg).

A new route and a new Colonial Coach operator appeared in November 1953 in the form of Skyways Ltd. and their fortnightly service from Stansted Airport to Malta and Cyprus. Avro Yorks were used and the flight to Malta took $7^1/_2$ hours, followed by a further $6^1/_2$ hours for the onward leg to Nicosia. From the end of 1954 the larger and much more comfortable Hermes 4 airliners replaced the Yorks and these were in turn superseded by Lockheed Constellations in 1959, by which time the departure point had been switched to London Airport. The fare at that time was £75 return. Skyways were taken over by Euravia in 1962 but the service continued until April 1964, using a Constellation which still retained Skyways markings.

Hunting-Clan introduced V.833 Visc turbo-props onto their Colonial Co services to Africa in July 1959. G-A illustrated was the first example to delivered.

Air Charter Ltd. introduced the forty-two-seat Supertrader conversion of the Avro Tudor design onto their own Colonial Coach service from Stansted to Idris and Lagos in 1954. In the same year Airwork and Hunting-Clan Air Transport (as the company was now called) opened another joint 'Safari' route, this time to Accra via Bordeaux, Tangier, Villa Cisneros, Dakar, Bathurst, Freetown and Abidjan. Vikings were once again used and nightstops were made at Tangier and Dakar on this twice-weekly operation. Mail was also carried from London to Dakar and Bathurst.

Hunting-Clan struck out alone with a new service to Gibraltar via Biarritz on 21 February 1955. This service was operated on a monthly basis, usually with the trusty Vikings, although Hunting-Clan's new Viscount turbo-props were used for some flights, but the service was terminated at the end of September.

Bovingdon Airport closed down in April 1956 and Hunting-Clan transferred their operating base to London Airport. In September 1957 they introduced pressurised Viscount 700 aircraft onto the Salisbury run which then became twice-weekly. Stops were made at Rome, Benina, Wadi Halfa or Luxor, Khartoum, Entebbe, Ndola and Lusaka. Viscounts also displaced the Vikings on the routing to Nairobi via Rome, Athens or Benina, Cairo or Wadi Halfa or Luxor, Khartoum and Entebbe.

More powerful Viscount 800s replaced Vikings on the joint Airwork/Hunting-Clan service to Accra on 6 January 1958, enabling the nightstops to be reduced to one (at Las Palmas) in each direction. By now these services had been redesignated as Tourist Class services, replacing the Colonial Coach operation.

On 4 October 1960 new low-fare 'Skycoach' services came into effect on the cabotage routes from London to East and Central Africa. They were operated jointly by BOAC, British United Airways, Central African Airways and East African Airways. Sixty-two-seat BUA Viscount 800s were used for these flights, which replaced the former cheap-fare Argonaut services of EAA and the 'Zambesi' service of CAA.

'Skycoach' services were also introduced to cabotage destinations in other areas of the world. On 10 October 1960 Cunard-Eagle Airways inaugurated the first 'Skycoach' service from London to Bermuda and Nassau, using 113-seat Britannia 310s. The Cunard-Eagle flights alternated with a similar BOAC service. The fare of £130 was only available to British residents and the two airlines split the revenue on a pro-rata basis.

In 1950, Hunting Air Travel commenced regular trooping services from Bovingdon to West Africa. One of their Vikings is seen here at Bovingdon, in company with Halifax G-AKEK and a South African-registered Dakota.

Chapter 9

Trooping Flights

The valuable role played by the independent airlines in the Berlin Airlift and other crises demonstrated their value as a military transport reserve and led to the awarding of Government contracts to them for the scheduled rotation of troops and their dependants between Britain and her military bases overseas in the 1950s. This activity was to last until the end of the decade, by which time the withdrawal of Britain from bases 'east of Suez' had restricted the operation of such flights to the support of forces based in Germany. At its peak in the mid-fifties however trooping-flight activity accounted for two-thirds of all the passenger-miles flown by the independent carriers.

One of the major operators of trooping flights was Hunting Air Travel (later to become Hunting-Clan Air Transport) who were awarded in June 1950 a War Office contract for approximately 60 flights to West Africa over a nine-month period. This contract had previously been held by Airwork Ltd. The first service departed from Hunting's Bovingdon base on 1 July 1950. Two Vickers Vikings were used for the flights, which took three days to reach their destination. A day's rest was scheduled in West Africa before the three-day trip back to Bovingdon. The contract was renewed in 1951 and an additional one was awarded for flights to Malta and Gibraltar over the next two years. Between August 1951 and October 1953 the Hunting Vikings made 1016 trips to Malta and 232 to Gibraltar, carrying 75,333 service personnel and families. Once again these contracts were renewed for a further two years from October 1953. 500 flights were specified for the carriage of over 30,000 passengers each year. At the time this represented about thirty per cent of the total number of trooping passengers flown each year by all the British independent operators combined. Hunting's operating base was transferred to London Airport in late 1954.

Other early trooping airlines were the Lancashire Aircraft Corporation, who flew Avro Yorks to the Egyptian Canal Zone, and Eagle Aviation who operated many flights to Singapore on behalf of the Air Ministry from 1951 onwards. Avro Yorks were again used for this contract and for another one Eagle were awarded in January 1952, this time for approximately forty flights to Rhodesia for each year of a two-year period. Eagle originally proposed using flying-boats for this service and negotiations were opened with the Ministry of Civil Aviation for the purchase of up to six Short Solents which would have been landed in the Victoria Falls area, but the deal fell through. Services actually started using Avro Yorks but on 25 November 1952 Eagle sold their York fleet to Skyways Ltd., along with the remaining fourteen months of the contract. During the period from 1 July 1951 to 30 June 1952 Eagle had carried 2,250 troops and 8,450 dependants.

Also in 1952 Airwork Ltd. were awarded an Air Ministry contract for flights from their base at Blackbushe Airport to Kenya and the Egyptian Canal Zone. To operate these services they purchased four Hermes 4 aircraft from BOAC. Because of the political situation at the time these sixty-eight seat aircraft wore military serials and RAF markings on the flights. Airwork followed up this operation in 1954 by winning another contract for almost three year's work carrying 7,000 troops each year between the UK and Singapore. Once again Hermes aircraft were employed on this contract, which was worth some £1.25m each year and was the largest single air trooping contract ever placed by the Air Ministry at that time.

Airwork used Hermes aircraft on numerous long-range trooping contracts in the 1950s. One of their fleet is seen here at Blackbushe.

Another airline to benefit from the military bases overseas was Scottish Airlines. During the period 1950-1 they had operated a monthly service to the Middle East on behalf of the NAAFI and had also carried service personnel and families in Dakotas. In 1952 they acquired the first of eight Avro Yorks. Three of these fifty-seater aircraft entered service in January 1953 carrying cadets from Stansted to Montreal for training in Canada. 1700 cadets were carried during 1953 and in 1954 trooping flights were also made to Malta, Cyprus and the Suez Canal Zone in Egypt. Because of the quasi-military nature of the Suez flights their crews were obliged to change into service uniforms during the Malta-Suez leg.

As mentioned previously, Skyways Ltd. acquired the remainder of the Eagle Aviation trooping contract to Rhodesia and their three Avro Yorks in November 1952. They were, however, already operating trooping flights in the opposite direction at that time, to Bermuda and Jamaica on behalf of the War Office. The service had commenced on 2 July 1952, with Avro York G-AHFD operating the first schedule. The two-year contract covered the carriage of 4,000 servicemen and dependants. The Yorks used on this marathon journey took twenty-seven hours to fly from the Skyways base at Bovingdon to Bermuda via Keflavik and Gander. They were configured to carry only thirty-six passengers as this was considered to be the maximum that could be safely transported over the range-critical 1370-mile sector between Keflavik and Gander. It was a Skyways York that unintentionally

Skyways Avro York G-AHFG at Manchester for repairs prior to continuing its trooping flight to Bermuda and Kingston on 29 November 1952 – the first ever trans-Atlantic flight from Manchester.

operated the very first trans-Atlantic flight from Manchester Airport on 29 November 1952, after diverting there with engine trouble three days earlier, whilst en route to Bermuda and Kingston. After repairs G-AHFG continued its trooping flight via Keflavik and Gander. In October 1952 Skyways moved their operating base to Stansted and with their arrival customs facilities were reinstated at the airport. At this time Skyways averaged one inbound and one outbound trooping flight each day but at busy periods this was doubled. During 1952 they carried more than 40,000 trooping passengers. Hermes aircraft replaced the Yorks on the Middle and Far East runs from September 1954 and in July 1955 the airline was awarded a contract worth more than £500,000 each year for the carriage of 12,000 passengers annually to Cyprus via Rome, using the Hermes fleet.

For some airlines the award of a lucrative trooping contract came just too late to save them from impending financial disaster. In April 1952 Crewsair secured a War Office contract for eighty flights over twelve months from Blackbushe to West Africa via Gibraltar using Vikings. The contract was worth £250,000 to Crewsair but after commencing the flights they were forced to suspend all operations in October 1952.

Eagle Aviation had several of their Vikings converted to a high-density layout by their associate company Eagle Aircraft Services during 1953. In this new configuration they were equipped with 36 aft-facing reclining seats and were used by Eagle to re-enter the trooping market in 1955. Known as 'Troopmasters', the revamped Vikings flew a large number of services from Blackbushe to Cyprus, Malta, Libya, the Egyptian Canal Zone and West Africa.

In September 1953 Freddie Laker's Aviation Traders Ltd. purchased from the Ministry of Civil Aviation a mixed fleet of various versions of the Avro Tudor airliner which had been rejected by BOAC and began a radical conversion programme to modify them for operation by Air Charter Ltd. The job lot as purchased consisted of four Mk.1s, two Mk.3s and four Mk.4s, plus eighty-eight spare Merlin engines. The end result of the programme was the Avro Supertrader, which incorporated major changes such as the removal of the pressurisation system, the installation of new heating and ventilation systems, modifications to the radio and electrics, the fitting of an additional emergency exit and the substitution of more modern wheels and propellors as well as upgrading of the passenger facilities. The Supertrader was awarded its Certificate of Airworthiness on 2 February 1954 after tests which had demonstrated an increase in performance over the original 1949 specifications. The first Supertrader trooping service was flown by G-AGRG from Stansted to Hamburg on 14 February 1954 and from then until 1958 these forty-two seat aircraft flew numerous trooping services to the Middle and Far East. The type was eventually retired after its last service on 16 June 1959. This was also the last flight of any Tudor variant in the world. Meanwhile, Air Charter had also commenced a Southend-Cyprus DC-4 operation in August 1956.

Britavia successfully tendered for a number of Air Ministry contracts in 1954 and purchased six Hermes 4 aircraft from BOAC to operate the flights. After delays caused by an industrial dispute involving BOAC engineering staff the Hermes airliners were eventually delivered to Blackbushe and entered service in July 1954 on runs to Singapore, Egypt, the Persian Gulf, Cyprus and Malta.

Modern turbo-prop equipment was introduced onto trooping services in October 1957 by Transair, who used two Viscount 800s on routes from London Airport to Benina, Gibraltar, Idris and Malta. Their aircraft were fitted out with fifty-eight-rear-facing seats and also featured a 'mothers' room' and a four-cot nursery on board for the convenience of service wives travelling with infants. The UK departure point was transferred to Gatwick airport when it re-opened in 1958. From there services continued until the merger of Transair into British United Airways in 1960.

The last trooping flight from Aden arrives at Stansted in the mid-1960s and passengers deplane from their British United Britannia.

In 1959 Eagle Aviation placed their fleet of three DC-6Cs onto trooping flights from Blackbushe to Aden, Nairobi and Nicosia, but by then the withdrawal of British forces from bases in the Middle and Far East was resulting in the termination of many long-running operations and few new contracts were being awarded. It was still possible however to pick up some business from trooping and on 1 October 1958 Air Charter Ltd. made the first of several trips from Stansted to Christmas Island in the Pacific, carrying up to 124 passengers each time in Britannia 300srs aircraft. On 5 February 1959 their Britannia 307 G-ANCE took off from Stansted with 100 military passengers bound for Adelaide and Sydney. On the return leg 112 passengers were uplifted at Christmas Island for the UK. The round-the-world trip of 26,100 miles was completed in $72^{1}/_{2}$ hours, travelling out via Bahrain, Ceylon and Singapore and returning via San Francisco and Montreal. Eagle Aviation also operated to Christmas Island, their Britannia 318 G-APYY making their first trip on 6 April 1960. Another Britannia operator to the Far East was Hunting-Clan Air Transport, who had been awarded an Air Ministry contract for six flights each month from London to Singapore and Hong Kong, the inaugural service leaving London Airport on 15 May 1959.

In the winter of 1960/1 Silver City Airways were operating Hermes aircraft from Manston in Kent to German bases under a contract that called for approximately fifty flights each month to Gutersloh, Hanover and Wildenrath. Following the merger of Silver City into the British United Airways group the departure point was changed to Gatwick.

On 2 October 1961 BUA were awarded a contract under which they became the sole carrier of British servicemen and their families to and from bases in West Germany. From this date the sea crossing from Harwich to the Hook of Holland was no longer used for this purpose. Viscount 800s and DC-6Cs were utilised for the flights from Gatwick and Manchester to Dusseldorf, Frankfurt, Gutersloh, Hanover and Wildenrath and 11,000 passengers were carried each month.

During 1964 BUA were still using Britannia aircraft for trooping but on the night of 1 October 1964 the last Britannia service left Stansted. From then on all BUA trooping flights to Africa and the Middle East were flown out of Gatwick by VC-10s equipped with 129 rear-facing seats on routes to Aden, Bahrain and Nairobi.

Chapter 10

Coach-Air and Rail-Air

The coach-air concept was a successful answer to the problem of providing low-cost travel to over-water tourist destinations whilst reducing considerably the overall time involved in journeys using steamships. Aircraft were used on the shortest possible sea crossing, with coaches providing surface connections at each end of the flight.

Much of the credit for the successful exploitation of the concept must go to Mr Eric Rylands, who introduced the system on the Blackpool-Isle of Man route of his Lancashire Aircraft Corporation in 1952. Coaches from various points fed passengers onto four Rapide flights each day across the Irish Sea and as a result the loads rose from 8,000 in 1951 to 12,000 in 1952. During 1954 Dakotas took over on the route and up to fourteen services a day were operated in the peak season. 18,500 passengers were carried that year. In 1956 the Lancashire Aircraft Corporation was absorbed into the northern division of Silver City Airways but by then Mr Rylands had left to join Skyways Ltd., taking his coach-air brainchild with him.

On 21 September 1955 Skyways operated special inaugural coach-air services between London and Paris in preparation for the start of regular schedules on 30 September. Coaches conveyed passengers from Victoria Coach Station in London to Lympne Airport in Kent, from where a fleet of four thirty-six seat Dakotas was used for the flights to Beauvais in northern France. From there more coaches completed the journey into the centre of Paris. The seating capacity of the coaches was matched to that of the aircraft and off-peak fares at that time were as low as £7.14.0 (£7.70) return.

Great emphasis was placed on the lucrative sale of duty-free goods on these services and to save time passengers were able to order and pay for their purchases at the Paris city terminal before boarding the coach to Beauvais. While they were on the road their orders were passed to the airport, where they were parcelled up ready for the cabin crew to distribute during the short flight. The new service was a success from the outset, with 47,000 passengers being carried during the first year of operation.

By the summer of 1957, sixteen flights each day were being operated and in that year a new route from London to Vichy via Lympne was inaugurated. This was the first British air service to Vichy since the pre-war operation of Hillmans Airways.

In May 1958 another new service, to Nice via Lyons Airport was opened and a special routing to Brussels via Antwerp Airport was operated for the duration of the Brussels International Exhibition.

A separate company known as Skyways Coach-Air was set up in October 1958 to take over responsibility for all the coach-air services. This company operated as an independent entity and thus was not included in the take-over of Skyways by Euravia in 1962.

Services continued virtually unchanged throughout the period 1959-1961 but a major benefit to the passengers was introduced on 17 April 1962 when the airline operated its first commercial service with the new Avro 748 turbo-prop airliner, on the Lympne-Beauvais route. Skyways Coach-Air was only the second airline in the world to operate the Avro 748, which they furnished in a forty-four seat configuration and which provided a faster and much smoother flight than the Dakotas could manage. By 1963 three examples were in service and two of the Dakotas were then converted for all-cargo operation.

Skyways Coach-Air Avro 748 G-ARMV was used on the Lympne-Beauvais route from 1962. The aircraft is pictured here at the 1964 Biggin Hill Air Fair.

During 1965 coach-air services were launched from provincial points with the opening of an East Midlands-Beauvais route. By this time however the national carriers BEA and Air France were responding to the demand for low-cost travel by introducing many cheap fares on their direct London-Paris flights and the price advantage of the coach-air operation was seriously eroded. Skyways Coach-Air was forced to cease operations in January 1971. The airline was briefly re-activated under the name of Skyways International but this new company was taken over in 1972 by Dan-Air who soon discontinued all coach-air operations.

From 1956 onwards Skyways had faced competition from Silver City Airways, who commenced their 'Silver Arrow' coach-air services to Paris and Brussels on 11 May. Coach transport was provided from central London to Lydd Airport near Dungeness and from there Bristol 170 Wayfarers carried passengers across the Channel. In the case of Paris-bound travellers their destination airport was Le Touquet and the twenty-minute flight was operated in conjunction with Silver City's French associate Cie Air Transport. A railcar provided onward transportation into Paris and the whole journey took 6 hours 50 minutes. Passengers for Brussels flew to Ostend and then completed their journey by coach. On 21 May 1958 the larger Mk 32 Superfreighters, converted to sixty-seat 'Super Wayfarer' configuration, were introduced on Lydd-Le Touquet flights.

Major changes were made to the 'Silver Arrow' services in 1959. The rundown elsewhere in government trooping flights had left Silver City's parent company Britavia with several redundant Hermes 4 airliners and the decision was taken to transfer some of these much larger aircraft to Silver City for use on the coach-air services. Runway restrictions at Lydd resulted in the relocation of the 'Silver Arrow' departure point to Manston Airport in Kent, with the first schedule being flown from there to Le Touquet on 15 June 1959.

In 1962 Silver City became part of the British United Airways group and that summer the 'Silver Arrow' service again moved its base, this time to Gatwick Airport. British United Viscount turbo-props replaced the elderly Hermes aircraft and instead of using coach connections the service became a rail-air operation, utilising the rail link from London's Victoria Station to Gatwick and the newly-improved rail connection from Le Touquet Airport into Paris.

Silver City Bristol Superfreighter G-AMWD at Southampton (Eastleigh) Airport on 4 September 1954, whilst embarking cars for a service to Cherbourg.

Chapter 11

Car Ferries

The era of the cross-Channel car ferry aircraft began on 13 July 1948 with the Silver City Airways inaugural flight from Lympne to Le Touquet in France, using Bristol 170 Freighter G-AGVC. Two cars were carried on this first flight and the rate charged for a car and four passengers was £32 one-way.

The service proved an immediate success, offering a speedy alternative to the tedious and sometimes rough sea passage across the English Channel and Silver City went on to acquire a fleet of Bristol 170s. During 1950 an enterprising London taxi owner utilised the Silver City car ferry link to offer his customers a London-Paris taxi service, using the same vehicle throughout. Silver City's traffic quickly grew and during August 1951 the airline carried $2^1/_2$ times more cargo (in the form of cars and two-wheeled vehicles) into Lympne than the combined totals at Northolt and London airports. On 1 July 1952 Silver City completed their 10,000th accident-free Channel crossing.

The Bristol 170s continued to plod their way across the Channel, operating at 1,000 feet southbound and 1,500 feet northbound and one of their captains in those days was Mr Adam Thomson, later to become famous as one of the founders of Caledonian Airways. Problems were being encountered with the grass airfield at Lympne though. On wet days there was the danger of heavily-laden aircraft skidding on landing or take-off and in February 1953 torrential rain rendered the surface virtually unusable, with aircraft digging deep ruts whilst taxying, and services were temporarily transferred to Southend. On 22 September further heavy rain caused chaos and some operations were transferred for a while to RAF West Malling. Lympne was owned at the time by the Ministry of Civil Aviation and Silver City were by far their biggest customer there. During 1952 they had paid £12,000 in landing fees but despite persistent campaigning no improvements had been carried out, so in 1953 the airline announced its intention of opening its own purpose-built car ferry airport near Dungeness.

Until this was ready Silver City continued to use Lympne, their loads over the Easter of 1953 being seven times greater than for the previous Easter period. The 1953 figures were helped by the introduction in April of two of the larger Bristol 170 Mk.32 Superfreighters. These could carry three cars and up to twenty passengers plus cycles and motor-cycles. The Superfreighters were also used to open a new route in May 1953, from Gatwick Airport to Le Touquet. The passenger fare for this forty-minute flight was £4 single or £7.4.0 (£7.20) return. Small cars were charged at £10.10.0 (£10.50) single, motor-cycles at £2.5.0 (£2.25), and bicycles at 7/6d

(37^1/$_2$p) each way. At the same time Silver City also introduced the world's shortest car-ferry flight. This was from Southampton (Eastleigh) to Bembridge (IOW). The journey time was nine minutes and up to twenty-four flights were operated each day. Silver City had commenced operations from Southampton (Eastleigh) in 1951 with a Bristol 170 service to Cherbourg. Jersey Airlines also used the same type of aircraft on a car-ferry link to Jersey but the absence of a hard runway at Eastleigh caused waterlogging problems in wet weather and Silver City eventually transferred their services to Bournemouth, returning in 1961 when a new owner took over at Southampton and plans were set in hand for a concrete runway.

On 13 July 1954 the new Ferryfield Airport at Lydd was opened by Silver City. This new airfield featured two concrete runways, a large terminal building and Decca 424 approach radar. Operations at Lympne were gradually transferred to Lydd and the last Silver City service out of Lympne departed for Le Touquet on 3 October 1954. The airport was then closed down on 31 October, but it was relicenced in 1955 by Skyways and used for their coach-air services, covered elsewhere in this book.

On 24 March 1955 Silver City began car-ferry operations across the Irish Sea with a proving flight from Castle Kennedy aerodrome at Stranraer to Newtownards, Belfast. Two cars were carried in a Bristol 170 Mk 21 and a regular thrice-daily service commenced on 6 April. The cost of transporting a car on the twenty-minute flight was £7 each way. A similar service was opened on 17 June 1955 between RAF Woodvale near Southport and Newtownards. The flying time on this longer routing was one hour.

In the meantime however Silver City's monopoly on the cross-Channel routes had been broken by Freddie Laker's Air Charter Ltd., who inaugurated a Southend-Calais car ferry service on 4 April 1955. Bristol 170 Mk 32 Superfreighters were used and six flights were operated on the first day. This route was supplemented from 18 October by another Air Charter service from Southend, this time to Ostend.

Silver City further expanded their Irish Sea network on 3 August 1956 when a daily service from Newtownards to the Isle of Man was inaugurated. Cars were carried at rates from £8.10.0 (£8.50) each way.

Rotterdam's new airport was opened on 1 October 1956 and Air Charter immediately commenced a twice-daily car ferry service from Southend. On 4 June 1957 Air Charter and SABENA inaugurated a joint operation between Southend and Ostend. A Bristol Superfreighter painted in the SABENA colour scheme was used on the thirty-nine minute crossing, carrying up to three cars plus sixteen passengers and two-wheeled vehicles. The initial frequency was six flights daily but this was doubled from July.

Silver City's services were also thriving at this time and during July 1957 the airline completed its 100,000th cross-Channel ferry flight. The success of the operation had made possible some drastic fare reductions. The 1957 off-season car rate between Lydd and Calais or Le Touquet was £6.10.0 (£6.50) single, compared to the £32 rate charged nine years earlier when the routes were opened. At the end of the year the rates were reduced again and it

became 4/- (20p) cheaper for owners of Austin A35-sized cars to fly them across with Silver City than to take them on the steamer. On 29 May 1959 Silver City carried their 250,000th car from Lydd to Le Touquet, eleven years after they first started car ferry services from Lympne.

Not all new car-ferry services were so successful though. During the summers of 1957 and 1958 Jersey Airlines operated 'Baronet' class Bristol 170s from Jersey to Dinard. The route proved uneconomical however and was then suspended.

Air Charter Ltd Bristol 170 Mk 32 Superfreighter G-AOUV at Southend in September 1957. The aircraft wears the SABENA colours used on their joint car-ferry service to Ostend. A Miles Gemini is parked outside the control tower.

On 25 February 1959 Air Charter Ltd. established Channel Air Bridge as an associate company to take over the operation of all their car ferry services.

Another Irish Sea routing came on-line on 25 April 1960 when BKS Air Transport inaugurated a daily Liverpool-Dublin Bristol 170 service. The frequency was increased to four times daily in the peak season but had to be withdrawn in 1961 because of the financial difficulties of BKS at the time. Aer Lingus re-opened the route with Aviation Traders Carvairs on 8 May 1962 and operated it until 1965 when the competition from new drive-on/drive-off sea ferries finally proved too much. Within days of opening the Liverpool-Dublin service Aer Lingus had also commenced new Carvair routes from Dublin to Bristol and from Cork to Bristol but these too were eventually withdrawn.

During 1961 Silver City Airways signed a pooling agreement with their French associate company Cie Air Transport and transferred three Superfreighters to them for use on Le Touquet-Lydd, Calais-Lydd and Cherbourg-Bournemouth services.

Early in 1962 Channel Air Bridge took delivery of their first Carvair aircraft. These could carry five cars instead of three and for the 1962 summer season the airline had three of them in service. Nevertheless they estimated that they still had to turn away $2^1/_2$ times as much traffic as they were able to carry.

During 1962 Silver City Airways became part of the British United Airways group of companies and on 1 January 1963 they were merged with Channel Air Bridge to form British United Air Ferries, with operating bases at Lydd, Southend and Southampton. At the time of its formation the constituent airlines of BUAF were at the peak of their success, and during the first two weeks of August 1963 traffic exceeded all previous records. Twenty-nine aircraft were used to carry 12,150 cars and 51,629 passengers on 4,762 Channel crossings, an average of 320 sectors per day. The average daily load for these weeks was 810 cars and 3,400 passengers. During the summer of 1963 the newly-introduced 'deep-penetration' routes to Basle, Geneva and Strasbourg showed the most spectacular growth. Carvair G-ASDC made the first landing of the type at Lydd on 13 December 1963.

New services inaugurated during 1964 included routes to Liege from Lydd and Southend, a Bristol Superfreighter operation between Coventry and Calais, and on 31 October the first use of a Carvair on the Jersey-Bournemouth routing.

Chapter 12

Ad Hoc Charter Flights

Although the lucrative inclusive-tour charters and trooping contracts provided a steady source of income for those operators fortunate enough to secure them, most of the charter airlines still had spare aircraft capacity which they attempted to fill with one-off or short-series charter flights worldwide.

One of the earliest exponents of long-distance passenger charters was William Dempster Ltd., which was formed in 1948 at Blackbushe Airport as a Rapide operator. In April 1950 a change of role took place when two former BSAAC Avro Tudors were purchased and used for low-fare tourist flights to South Africa. These aircraft were initially fitted out as fifty-two seaters and the fares charged were a fraction of the scheduled air fare. The flights to Johannesburg continued throughout 1950 and 1951 from both Blackbushe and Bovingdon. To supplement the Tudors the airline sometimes chartered Dakotas from Pan African Air Charter. In September 1951 the operating base was changed to Stansted but at the end of 1953 all operations were suspended and the one surviving Tudor was sold to Aviation Traders Ltd. as a source of spares for their Supertrader conversion programme.

A few charter airlines were still making do with converted bombers such as the Handley Page Halifax at the beginning of the 1950s. By 1950 the Lancashire Aircraft Corporation was one of these few operators but their three aircraft were much in demand for cargo flights to Milan, carrying supplies of penicillin on the outward leg and returning to their Bovingdon base laden with imported textiles. The aircraft were also sub-contracted by BOAC for cargo flights to Singapore and Tokyo. With the demise of the last Eagle Aviation Halifax in November 1950, LAC became the sole commercial operator of the type. In 1951 several trips were made to Buenos Aires, Hong Kong and Bangkok but the Halifaxes were finally retired at the end of the year.

War surplus Dakotas were readily available at this time and were used by many fledgling operators such as Crewsair, who flew their first charter on 23 March 1950, carrying an aircraft engine from Dunsfold to Basra. Crewsair subsequently flew many textile charters from Lille to their base at Southend on behalf of Lep Air Services. In its first eight weeks of service their single Dakota flew 350 hours. Crewsair later acquired a second example and by the end of October 1950 the two aircraft had amassed over 1500 hours in Crewsair service. The company also operated Vickers Vikings and on 6 November 1951 one of these carried seventeen passengers to the ceremonial opening of the new airport at Entebbe in Uganda. At the end of October though Crewsair ceased operations altogether. Some of its founders were soon to be involved in the creation of BKS Aero Charter, the predecessor of BKS Air Transport.

One of the most useful aircraft for carrying bulky loads over long distances was the Avro York and among the first to appreciate its potential was Mr Freddie Laker. In 1950 his Aviation Traders company bought a selection of damaged Yorks and Lancaster bombers and used the components from nine Yorks and three Lancasters to construct three Yorks in first-class condition. With these Mr Laker formed the airline Air Charter Ltd. and used them on a second Berlin Airlift in August 1951, caused by Russia's interference with the flow of exports from Berlin factories to the West.

Also involved with Avro Yorks in 1950 was another airline entrepeneur Mr Harold Bamberg, the founder of Eagle Aviation Ltd. Eagle bought three York aircraft from BOAC in 1950 and used them for cargo work and passenger charters, for which purpose they were furnished with either thirty or forty-six seats. Initially the Yorks were based at Bovingdon before moving to Aldermaston and then again on 1 April 1950 to Luton Airport. They were joined in December by three more Yorks which had been purchased from Argentina for £9,000 each. Many long-haul flights were made and on 3 October 1952 an Eagle Aviation York left Luton on that was to become the longest charter flight ever undertaken by a British operator at the time. The first leg carried thirty Alsatian dogs from London and Dusseldorf to Karachi for the Government of Pakistan. At Karachi twenty cattle replaced the dogs as cargo and these were flown via Aden, Khartoum, Kano, Dakar and Natal to Beltera in Brazil. The aircraft then returned to Karachi to pick up a further twenty head of cattle and carry them also to Beltera. After unloading there for the second time the York positioned back to Luton to end a trip that had covered 37,000 miles. In November 1952 however the Eagle Aviation fleet of Yorks was sold to Skyways Ltd. for £160,000 including spares.

Three of Eagle Aviation's Avro Yorks outside the original control tower at Luton Airport in 1951/2. On the right of the picture is an RAF Percival Pembroke.

The festivities for Coronation Year in 1953 provided a unique opportunity for the public to participate in a series of one-hour 'aerial cruises', flying in one of Aquila Airways' flying-boats over the vast naval fleet lined up for inspection by Her Majesty The Queen in Southampton Water.

In 1954 the Federated Fruit Company set up its own cargo airline known as Federated Air Transport to fly large quantities of mushrooms from Dublin to Liverpool for onward distribution by road to markets throughout the North of England. Two Avro Ansons and a Rapide were used on the 'mushroom airlift', and on the return legs the aircraft carried newspapers to Dublin and the Isle of Man. The service remained in operation until February 1961 when new licencing regulations were introduced which would have greatly increased the company's overheads. Federated Air Transport was then closed down, but the mushrooms still made the journey by air, aboard the freight services of Aer Lingus.

In the late 1950s, the Dan-Air fleet of Avro Yorks was used on long-range charters to the Far East and Africa from Blackbushe, where G-ANTI was photographed.

Another operator of the Avro York was Dan-Air Services, who used three examples on cargo flights from their Blackbushe base to Africa and the Far East from January 1955. The Yorks had a useful eight-ton payload and were fitted with large cargo doors. These features helped Dan-Air to secure an Air Ministry contract for the carriage of stores from RAF Lyneham to Singapore in 1956. Two more Yorks were obtained and used on this and other contracts for many years. In 1959 the Singapore contract came to an end but Dan-Air were soon awarded another one by the Air Ministry, this time for the transportation of 'Black Knight' research rockets from the UK to the Woomera rocket range in Australia. To fulfil this contract a Bristol 170 Freighter was purchased and placed onto the flights which took twelve days in each direction. When available the Yorks were also sometimes used on this run, until the last example was eventually retired early in 1964.

Also based at Blackbushe was the Britavia fleet of Hermes 4 airliners. One of these became the first Hermes to fly the North Atlantic when G-ALDU carried thirty-nine seamen from Blackbushe to New York via Shannon and Gander in a total time of 17 hours 15 minutes on 14 November 1955.

Meanwhile, up at Burnaston Airport at Derby, the close proximity of Derby Aviation's base to the Rolls-Royce aero-engine factory ensured a steady flow of charter assignments for their Dakota fleet from 1955 onwards, carrying engine parts and technicians to destinations as far afield as India.

The Royal Tour of Nigeria by HM The Queen in 1956 provided extra revenue for Transair Ltd., who provided three of their Dakotas as support aircraft for the twenty-eight day tour. The aircraft left London Airport in January and completed over 50,000 miles without any serious serviceability problems.

A major refugee airlift was mounted in 1956 in the aftermath of the Hungarian Uprising. Thousands of Hungarians who had taken refuge in Austria were evacuated to the United Kingdom in an operation involving several British independent airlines. Blackbushe was designated as the arrival point for the flights, many of which were provided free or at cost price by the operators. On the outbound leg blankets, food, medical supplies and clothing were flown into Vienna and Linz airports. The first flight left Blackbushe on 16 November 1956 and by the time the airlift ended on 14 December some 7,000 refugees had been flown out of Austria. The last flight was performed by Cambrian Airways, whose Dakotas had made sixteen round trips. Dan-Air used two Dakotas to make eleven trips and BKS flew thirteen Viking sorties. Other airlines taking part included Silver City Airways and their subsidiary Air Kruise, whose Dakotas made twenty-six trips, and Derby Aviation, also using Dakotas to carry over 600 passengers on eighteen round trips. The airline which made the biggest contribution though was Eagle Aviation, whose Vikings made thirty-six round trips and brought out over 1200 refugees.

Skyways Ltd. had often operated freight flights to the Far East for BOAC and by 1957 they were providing a regular service to Singapore with Avro Yorks. In June 1959 Constellations were lease-purchased from BOAC to take over the Corporation's freight runs to Hong Kong, Singapore and Sydney. By 31 March 1962 however BOAC had sufficient cargo capacity on their own aircraft and the contract with Skyways was terminated.

During the late 1950s BKS Air Transport had begun to specialise in the carriage of racehorses around the UK and from 1958 onwards their Bristol 170s were frequently used for this purpose. One such aircraft was G-AMLJ which had been specially converted to carry six horses. During 1963 almost 3,000 animals were transported to race meetings throughout Britain and the Continent and in November 1964 Airspeed Ambassador G-ALZR was delivered to the BKS Bloodstock Division at Dublin after a conversion programme lasting eighteen months. The work had been carried out by BKS Engineering at Southend Airport and included the replacement of Rolls-Royce Tyne turbo-prop test-bed engines with the original Centaurus piston engines and the fitting of large cargo double doors. The Ambassador started to earn its keep in December 1964 when it carried race-horses into Cambridge Airport for the December Sales at Newmarket. The Bristol 170s were also still available as back-ups for this type of work.

From mid-1959 onwards DC-4 aircraft of Air Charter Ltd. had been used for transporting Jindivik target drones from Stansted to the rocket ranges in Australia, and Eagle Aviation's DC-6Cs had also been contracted to carry out similar Air Ministry freight flights to the Far East and Australia. They were joined in this work in 1960 by a Britannia 318 operating under the new company name of Cunard-Eagle Airways, following a merger with the famous steamship line. On 8 June 1962 one of the DC-6Cs inaugurated a new series of Air Ministry flights to Adelaide. The DC-6Cs were replaced in April 1964 by two Britannias which had been converted to feature the large cargo doors fitted to the RAF Britannias. This contract was to continue in operation until the collapse of the airline, by then known as British Eagle International Airlines, in November 1968.

A famous airliner of its day finally ended its career on 13 December 1964 when Hermes 4 G-ALDA of Air Links landed at Gatwick after a charter flight from Karachi and Brindisi, thus completing the last ever commercial flight by a Handley Page Hermes.

Following the loss of their BOAC contract in 1962, Skyways had secured a contract with Pan American Airways for the provision of a York freighter aircraft on permanent stand-by at London Airport. This aircraft was used to carry urgently needed spare parts and engines to Pan American aircraft stranded by unserviceability anywhere between Iceland and Iran. Skyways last York G-AGNV was to continue to carry out this duty until the end of 1964, when it was presented to an aircraft museum.

An attempt to start a completely new British cargo airline using far from new Constellation aircraft was initiated in 1964 by Aviation Charter Enterprises (or ACE Freighters as it was usually known). The company claimed to be Europe's first all-cargo airline and commenced operations on 1 March 1964. The Constellations were fitted with large rear freight doors and were joined later in the year by two DC-4 freighters. Several Ministry of Defence contracts were awarded for flights from RAF Lyneham and RAF Abingdon to the Middle and Far East. Also that year ACE Freighters acquired all four of the remaining South African Airways Constellations, but on 14 September 1966 the airline went into liquidation, ending Constellation operations in Britain.

G-AKBH was one of many Eagle Airways Vikings used for holiday charters in the early 1960s.
In this view taken at London Airport, a Dan-Air York and several BEA aircraft are also visible.

Chapter 13

Inclusive Tour Charters

The concept of matching up a planeload of aircraft seats with a block of hotel rooms to form a package tour was practised on an ad hoc basis by various charter airlines during the early post-war years, but one of the first examples of integrated tour operator/airline operations was started in 1952 by the Liverpool-based Cathedral Touring Agency and the local airline Starways, which were both owned by Liverpool businessman Mr J. H. Wilson, and whose first joint operations were pilgrimage tours to Lourdes in Dakota aircraft. These trips proved popular from the outset and were to be operated for many years to come. In 1953 the consortium diversified into general holiday tour operation when they inaugurated flights from Liverpool to Bilbao. By 1958 the Lourdes pilgrimage flights were operating on six days each week, with many of them using larger DC-4 aircraft. The holiday charters also flourished and by 1961 Starways were flying Dakotas and DC-4s from Liverpool to Basle, Biarritz, Malaga, Munich, Oporto and Palma and from Glasgow to Oporto and Lourdes. In that year turbo-prop Viscounts were first used for many of these flights. When British Eagle absorbed Starways on 1 January 1964 they did not acquire the Starways aircraft fleet. Consequently they purchased three DC-4 aircraft in 1964 specifically to operate the Starways inclusive-tour contracts from Manchester and Liverpool. The following year British Eagle's own Viscounts replaced the DC-4s on this work.

Meanwhile the holiday tour market was providing opportunities for more airlines to develop during 1953. Southend was a popular departure point in view of its proximity and therefore short flying time to the Continent, and a favourite destination at the time was Calvi in Corsica. BKS Aero Charter flew two Dakota services each week on behalf of Horizon Holidays, as part of a package deal that offered a fourteen-day holiday for just under £40. Dan-Air also operated their first ever inclusive tour flights from Southend to Calvi and in later years added Blackbushe as a departure point, again using Dakotas.

In 1955 Harold Bamberg of Eagle Aviation borrowed £50,000 and acquired the Sir Henry Lunn travel agency chain so that he could package his own tours and provide work for some of the fourteen Viking aircraft he had earlier purchased from BEA for a total price of £420,000. During the summer months tours were operated to Spain and Italy and in the winter the destinations served changed to Innsbruck and other winter sports resorts. Initially all the flights departed from Blackbushe but for the

1956 season Eagle operated their first provincial departures, from Manchester and Birmingham to Palma, again on behalf of the Sir Henry Lunn organisation. Eagle continued to use Blackbushe as their main base until the closure of that airport in May 1960 caused them to switch services to London Airport.

Other major operators of holiday charters in the mid-1950s included Transair, who offered Dakota flights from their base at Croydon Airport to Alghero, Barcelona, Basle, Lourdes, Madrid, Nice, Perpignan, Turin and Venice, and Air Kruise Ltd., who in 1956 had the most extensive holiday flight programme of any UK airline. Their fleet of Dakotas and Bristol 170 Wayfarers was leased from their associate company Silver City Airways and flew tour flights to all the major Mediterranean resorts from Manchester and Birmingham as well as their operating bases at Lydd and Blackbushe. It was an Air Kruise Dakota which operated the very first inclusive-tour flight out of Manchester Airport, carrying holidaymakers to Ostend on behalf of Sheffield United Tours on 29 May 1955. In 1958 the airline was absorbed into Silver City Airways and lost its own identity.

Overseas Aviation was formed as a charter operator at Southend in 1957 and from 1958 onwards the company used a fleet of Vikings and ex-BOAC Argonauts on an extensive programme of tour flights, initially from Southend and from 1960 onwards from their new base at Gatwick Airport. By the 1961 season Overseas Aviation was one of Europe's largest charter operators, flying from Belfast, Birmingham, Prestwick, Gatwick and Manchester, where up to four Argonauts were in use at busy weekends. That year they purchased eleven Canadair North Star aircraft from Trans-Canada Air Lines. Like the almost-identical Argonauts these were equipped to carry seventy passengers. At the peak of the 1961 season Overseas were second only among the independents to British United Airways in terms of fleet size but at the end of August the airline collapsed with debts in excess of £500,000.

Tradair Ltd. was also launched in 1957 and likewise commenced operations from Southend in 1958 but unlike other airlines they were to continue to be based there throughout their existence. Their initial fleet of Vikings was supplemented in July 1958 by three more which had previously been operated by the Queen's Flight of the RAF and must surely have been in superb condition for second-hand aircraft. For the 1959 season Tradair had seven Vikings in service on a network of routes from Southend and in February 1960 they took the bold step of purchasing two Viscount 700 turbo-prop airliners from Aer Lingus. These served alongside the Vikings for the next three years but the airline eventually fell into financial difficulties and in November 1962 their operations and their Viscount aircraft were taken over by Channel Airways, who were also based at Southend. Channel continued to operate holiday charters from there and soon supplemented the original Viscounts with several more purchased from BEA. Channel's Viscounts were fitted with seventy-one seats, almost certainly the highest-density seating arrangement used by any Viscount 700 operator.

Former Tradair Viking G-APOP, which was operated by Channel Airways on inclusive-tour flights in the early 1960s. It is seen here at Manchester Airport on 21 June 1964.

Dan-Air continued to expand their inclusive-tour operations from Blackbushe, placing a forty-four seat Bristol Wayfarer into service alongside the Dakotas in 1959. That same year the airline flew its first holiday charter from Manchester Airport and also acquired their first three Airspeed Ambassadors. These were converted back to their original BEA forty-nine seat layout and from 1960 used on services from various provincial airports and from Gatwick, which had become the Dan-Air operating base on the closure of Blackbushe in May.

Also using Manchester for holiday flights in 1959 was Hunting-Clan Air Transport who were operating a large programme of tours with DC-6C and Viscount aircraft.

Yet another new inclusive-tour airline to be formed in 1959 was Air Safaris, who had previously operated low-cost charter flights to South Africa under the name of African Air Safaris. Late in the year they moved their base from Southend to Gatwick and for the following summer they concentrated on holiday flights using a fleet of four Vikings and a single Hermes. By the summer of 1961 the Hermes fleet had increased to four aircraft and these bore the brunt of a programme of flights out of Birmingham, Bournemouth, Glasgow, Manchester and Newcastle as well as Gatwick. When loads were light however the smaller Vikings were sometimes substituted. It was one of the Air Safaris fleet that operated the first Hermes holiday charter from Newcastle Airport, to Palma on 21 May 1961. Tour flights were carried out from Newcastle on behalf of Airways Holidays and Horizon Travel but at the end of October 1961 Air Safaris ceased operations, owing over £521,000.

A Hermes of another charter operator, Falcon Airways, made aviation history in a small way on 9 October 1960 when it came to grief in the first aircraft accident in the UK to be officially attributed to aquaplaning. The aircraft G-ALDC overshot the runway on landing at Southend and ended up across a railway embankment with its tail nearly touching overhead power lines. Nobody was seriously hurt in this lucky escape but Falcon Airways too were to suffer financial failure at the end of the 1961 season.

One of the tour companies that had flights contracted out to both Falcon Airways and Air Safaris was Universal Sky Tours. Worried that the failure of these airlines and the prevailing poor image of the charter airlines as a whole could damage his own company's reputation, Captain Ted Langton of Universal Sky Tours decided that the best way to ensure control over the quality and cost of the flights was to form his own airline. This was the beginning of what was to become Britannia Airways. However, as Britain's entry into the EEC seemed to be imminent at that time, the name selected for the new airline was Euravia and the company was registered as such on 1 December 1961.

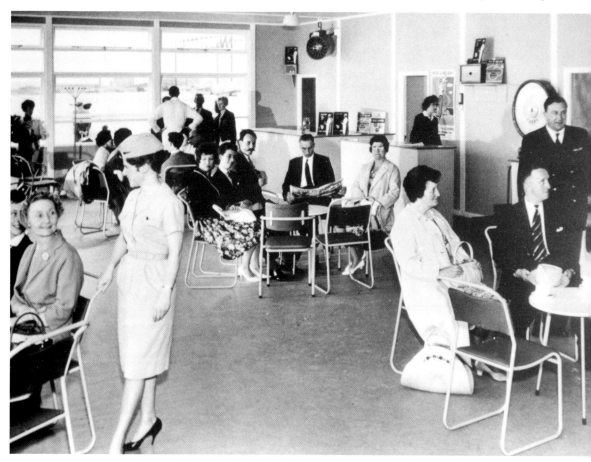

The interior of the passenger terminal at Luton Airport in the early 1960s.

A fleet of three L-049 Constellations was purchased from El Al Israel Airlines for £90,000, fully overhauled and equipped to carry eighty-two passengers. Euravia initially wanted to operate out of Gatwick but they were told that they would not be allowed any facilities of their own and all aircraft handling, maintenance, passenger handling and catering would have to be sub-contracted to one of the airlines already resident there. They then went to look at Luton Airport which had recently been linked to London by the new M1 Motorway. Customs facilities had been available at Luton since 1951 and a new control tower had been opened in September 1952. Euravia were offered the use of a new empty hangar and the airport owners Luton Corporation promised to extend the very small wooden terminal to accommodate 200 passengers in time for the 1962 season. By that time a new Decca radar system would also be operational at the airport. No duty-free shop existed at Luton at that time so Euravia had a monopoly on the sale of such goods to their passengers. They set up a town terminal in a former Avon tyre factory near Euston Station and provided coach transportation to connect with their flights. At this early stage in their aircraft fleet development they opted to share a hangar with Vauxhall Motors who used their portion to store car components manufactured at their nearby factory.

The very first commercial flight made by Euravia took place on 5 May 1962. Constellation G-ARVP positioned empty from Luton to Manchester from where it carried holidaymakers to Palma via Perpignan. That same year Euravia had an early opportunity to expand by taking over the financially troubled airline Skyways Ltd. They were able to purchase Skyways, which was Britain's largest charter airline at the time, for the nominal sum of £1, but they also had to take over Skyway's £1¼ million overdraft. The deal added three L-749 Constellations to their fleet and shortly afterwards another arrangement was agreed with the receivers of Trans-European Aviation for the lease of their two Constellations for £20 per flying hour, along with contracts for a guaranteed minimum of 600 flying hours per year.

On 20 May 1962, a Euravia Constellation operated the inaugural Universal Sky Tours charter from Liverpool Airport. This was to Valencia and was the first holiday charter to be operated from Liverpool by someone other than Starways or Aer Lingus. During 1962 Euravia carried less than 20,000 passengers but during the following year over 50,000 holidaymakers were flown to the sun from Luton, Manchester, Cardiff, Blackpool and Newcastle. The first service from Newcastle was operated by Constellation G-ALAL to Valencia on 19 May and Euravia and its successor Britannia Airways have been operating continuously from there since then.

The Constellations were replaced in 1964 by six former BOAC Britannia 102s which had been in storage at Cambridge Airport for some time. The price paid for the six aircraft was less than the new cost of a single Britannia srs 312 and even included engine spares. To highlight the introduction of this turbo-prop airliner the company name was changed to Britannia Airways on 16 August 1964. The Britannias seated 112 passengers and incorporated galleys that enabled Britannia Airways to become the first British holiday

charter airline to provide hot meals (usually cottage pie!) in flight. The inaugural service by the Britannia aircraft left Luton on 6 December 1964 bound for Tenerife and in 1965 Britannia Airways and Universal Sky Tours became part of the world-wide Thomson Organisation.

Developing alongside Euravia at Luton in the early 1960s was Autair who were operating Dakota charter flights during 1961. In 1962 Vikings replaced the Dakotas on inclusive-tour flights to a wide range of destinations and from 1964 Airspeed Ambassadors took over on the holiday routes.

The demise of Overseas Aviation in 1961 enabled Derby Airways to take over five of their Argonaut aircraft. Two were cannibalised for spares at Burnaston Airport, Derby, and the remaining three went into service on inclusive-tour flights from Manchester, Birmingham, Bristol and Cardiff. These aircraft were equipped to carry sixty-two passengers in pressurised comfort and their maximum range of 3880 miles brought all the major resort areas within easy reach. Because of airfield limitations they could not be operated commercially from the grass runways at Burnaston but they returned there frequently for overhauls and crew training sorties. Despite taking off and landing virtually empty they still made a terrible mess of the grass surface and it was common practice among the pilots to align the aircraft wheels along existing ruts to avoid further damage.

25 May 1953 at Luton Airport. Passengers board Euravia Constellation G-ARXE for a holiday charter flight. The aircraft still wears its former Skyways colour scheme. Sharing the apron is Derby Airways Argonaut G-ALHG. McAlpine Aviation's executive aircraft hangar is prominent in the background.

More new routes and aircraft were introduced during 1963. Channel Airways operated a programme of tours from Manchester to Ostend that year using DC-4 G-ARYY into which they had managed to fit eighty-eight seats, double the number carried in DC-4s when they first entered passenger service in the early post-war years. The acquisition of ex-BEA Viscount 701s enabled Cambrian Airways to enter the inclusive-tour market in earnest and an extensive schedule of flights was operated from 1963 onwards out of Cardiff and Bristol airports on behalf of local tour company Hourmont Holidays.

An Autair Ambassador arrives on its stand at Luton Airport, circa 1964. In the background are excavations for the present terminal complex. The contemporary terminal building in use at that time is just out of sight, to the left of the picture.

Still more new airlines were entering the holiday tour market at this time. In 1964 Air Links operated a programme from Gatwick using a small fleet of Argonauts and the world's only remaining airworthy Hermes 4. The Hermes was actually to outlast the Argonauts which were retired at the end of 1965.

Down at Manston Airport in Kent Air Ferry flew to more than twenty European destinations during 1963 and 1964 with Viking and DC-4 equipment. Another new airline to use Manston as its base was Invicta Airways, which operated its first revenue flight from there to Basle on 20 March 1965. During that summer Invicta flew from Manston to many tourist resorts using two DC4s and two Vikings.

Larger, pressurised equipment such as the DC-6B was now coming into service with operators such as Caledonian Airways, who commenced inclusive-tour operations in 1964. A typical trip for one of their DC-6Bs took 6 hours 30 minutes for the round trip from Gatwick to Palma. In the month of May 1964 592,000 Britons travelled on inclusive-tour flights, 397,000 on British carriers and the remainder on continental airlines such as the Alitalia subsidiary SAM and the Spanish company Spantax.

By 1965 British United Airways were able to offer holiday travellers such relatively modern aircraft as the Britannia srs 300 for their journey. These aircraft could cover the distance from Gatwick to Palma in 2 hours 15 minutes, cruising at 390 mph, and a fourteen-day holiday in a first-class hotel in Majorca could be offered for sale for £50-£60. Out of this package price the round-trip flight accounted for only £18, which was less than half the fare by scheduled flight. In the summer of 1965 over three million passengers travelled on 50,000 inclusive-tour flights from British airports.

Air Links replaced their single Hermes with a fleet of four Canadair Argonauts in 1964. G-ALHI is parked close to the site of the present-day South Terminal Satellite Building at Gatwick.

Air Ferry used Vikings on inclusive-tour flights from Manston in Kent from 1963 to 1966. G-AIVD was one of the aircraft used.

Stinson Reliant G-AFVT was painted dark blue and silver when seen here at Kidlington on 26 April 1959. In the distance is a Rapide.

Chapter 14

General Aviation

Although the term 'general aviation' is a comparatively recent invention all the various elements that comprise non-airline commercial aviation were present at the start of the 1950s. Strict import restrictions made it difficult and expensive to bring foreign-built aircraft into the UK and so almost all the aircraft in use were of British manufacture. This was not too much of a handicap initially as there was a plentiful supply of war-surplus trainers and communications types to provide the backbone of the post-war charter and flying club fleets.

At the beginning of the decade the majority of the British public had not flown before and almost every airfield had one or two companies offering pleasure flights. One of the most famous was Island Air Services. They had commenced operations from Croydon Airport in 1947 and had opened another base at Northolt the following year. At both these airports they offered trips in Rapide aircraft. Then in early 1948 they gained the concession for pleasure flying at London Airport, which was still in its infancy at the time. Tickets were sold from an ex-RAF caravan parked near the public enclosure. Flying was restricted to Sundays only but even so by the early 1950s the company had four Rapides making up to 100 flights each Sunday for six months of the year. These aircraft flew from 10am until dusk, carrying nine passengers aloft each time. The turnround time between flights averaged thirty seconds and at peak periods the four Rapides would take off in box formation across the main runway, using a taxiway as a take-off strip. They would then climb to 1,000ft, making a five-minute circuit of the airport and land on the main runway one behind the other, turning off at different intersections. The cost of this experience was 11/- (55p). Also on offer were longer sightseeing flights over London at 1500ft for 22/- (£1.10). Each pilot averaged six short flights or three of the longer ones in an hour.

Island Air Services had to pay £3,000 cash in advance to the airport authorities for each season's concession, plus landing and parking fees yet they still made a twenty per cent profit on the operation. During the 1955 season they made a clear profit of £10,000 and at one point they had to charter two fifty-two seat Elizabethan airliners from BEA to clear the backlog of passengers. Among the celebrities carried on the London sightseeing flights was the actress Miss Elizabeth Taylor, who was expecting her first baby at the time and had an urge to see her London flat from the air.

By 1956 however the increase in the numbers and landing speeds of the airliners using London Airport led the authorities to decide that the Island Air

Services flights were an air traffic control hazard and all pleasure flying was banned at the airport.

Throughout the 1950s pleasure flying flourished elsewhere though, particularly at seaside resorts. One of the longest established operators was Giro Aviation who had begun flying from Birkdale Sands airstrip on Southport Beach in 1938. Two Fox Moth biplanes were used and after the war's end the same two aircraft restarted the activity from the same site. One of them was ditched in the sea off Southport at the end of the 1956 season but the surviving example continued to provide flights until the expiry of its Certificate of Airworthiness in 1964. At that time Giro Aviation ceased operations but since then the beach at Southport has been used for the same purpose by several other operators.

PASSENGER CERTIFICATE

The certificate presented to passengers on Giro Aviation's Fox Moth pleasure flights from Southport Beach in the early 1950s.

This is to Certify

That the holder has flown in a De Havilland Fox Moth Air Liner.

Pilot.

The Giro Aviation Co. Ltd., of Southport, has been established since 1920 and up to the present time have carried 250,000 aerial passengers.

THE GIRO AVIATION Co. Ltd., BIRKDALE SANDS and HESKETH PARK AERODROMES, Southport.

G-ACCB

AIR CHARTER PASSENGER FLIGHTS; FLYING SCHOOL; AND AEROPLANE SALES.

The reverse of the Giro Aviation joyride passenger certificate, depicting a Fox Moth biplane at Birkdale Sands Aerodrome, Southport Beach. This aircraft was ditched in the sea off Southport in 1956.

G-ADDI, one of two DH Dragons used by Air Navigation and Trading for pleasure flying at Blackpool, is seen here at Squires Gate in July 1961.

A little further north at Blackpool Airport there were no fewer than five different concerns offering joy-rides in 1951. One of these was Air Navigation and Trading, who used two De Havilland Dragons for flights over the beach and around Blackpool Tower from 1951 until these aircraft were retired in 1962. The company then switched to Rapide equipment, supplemented for the 1962 season only by a Percival Prentice.

A relatively late starter in the pleasure flying business was Chrisair, which was founded early in 1961 by Mr and Mrs Chris Roberts. Rather unusually they did not choose a seaside location but spent the 1961 and 1962 seasons flying from Luton Airport, initially using a Leopard Moth and then a Percival Proctor. At the end of the 1962 season they moved their base to Ramsgate aerodrome, from where they had already been giving pleasure flights since 1961 at a price of 10/- (50p) per head. In November 1962 Chrisair purchased G-ADDI, one of two De Havilland Dragons formerly used by Air Navigation and Trading at Blackpool. This aircraft was operated from Ramsgate and then, from June 1963, from their new base at Northampton (Sywell) airfield. The Dragon soon became a familiar sight at airshows around the country, providing pleasure flights until its C.of A. expired in May 1968. At the end of the 1968 season Chrisair ceased operations permanently.

During the early 1950s several civilian operators were involved in Army Cooperation flights. These were usually operated as part of defence exercises such as 'Operation Emperor' in October 1950. A number of aircraft were chartered to ferry military personnel around the country and to play the part of 'hostile bombers' in the exercise. Among the aircraft used in this way were several Cambrian Air Services Rapides and no fewer than eight Rapides of the Lancashire Aircraft Corporation, representing an enemy bomber force.

Flying clubs were flourishing everywhere at this time. One which had an interesting sideline was the Wrafton Flying Club, which was formed in 1950 at RAF Chivenor in North Devon. The club operated two Austers and a Rapide and these were also used on a daily year-round service between Chivenor and Lundy Island in the middle of the Bristol Channel. Mail, passengers, beer and other essentials were ferried across to Lundy and pleasure flying was also carried out from Chivenor during the summer months. In 1952 the club was taken over by the North Devon Flying Club but the service to Lundy continued as usual. In December 1952 the run to Lundy was again taken over, this time by Devonair and a Miles Aerovan was acquired for use on this service in 1955. From 1960 onwards, however, Devonair's operations were gradually transferred to Coventry Airport. By 1962 the flights to Lundy had ceased and the company then concentrated on maintenance work at Coventry under the name of Light Aircraft Servicing Ltd.

Airviews Rapide G-AGOM at Newmarket Racecourse, circa 1956. The line-up of coaches in the background would suggest that a race meeting was in progress.

Another long-established flying club in the West Country was the Plymouth and District Aero Club, which had been founded in 1929 and resumed operations after the war. By 1951 the membership stood at over 300 and the aircraft fleet consisted of two Austers and single examples of the Miles Gemini and Messenger and De Havilland Tiger Moth. The Gemini was also available for charter work and the club continued to expand throughout the 1950s and 1960s.

Another popular and well-supported activity was air racing and in those days there were many more races than we are accustomed to today. The Lancashire Aircraft Corporation entered Percival Proctor G-AIHD in both the Air League Challenge Cup Trophy Race and the Yorkshire Aeroplane Club Trophy Race on 22 July 1950 at Sherburn-in Elmet aerodrome. Flown by LAC's Operations Manager, the Proctor came first in the Air League race at an average speed of 161mph. They also entered the same aircraft and pilot in the Daily Express International Air Race, which was flown along a stretch of the South coast from Hurn Airport. Bournemouth to Herne Bay on 16 September 1950. A total of sixty-seven aircraft started the race and sixty-one of these completed the course. The prize money totalled £2350 and the field included several Hawk Trainer Mk 3s and Proctors, Hurricane IIC G-AMAU, Airspeed Consul VX587, two Miles Aerovans, the Mamba-powered Miles Marathon G-AHXU and the LAC-entered Halifax bomber G-AKEC 'Air Voyager'. Piloted by LAC's Bovingdon Station Manager Capt. A. N. Marshall, the Halifax averaged 267mph but could only finish twenty-fourth. This was almost certainly the only occasion on which a Halifax had taken part in an air race! The actual winner was Proctor G-AHUZ.

G-AHKV, the Rapide used by the Automobile Association for traffic spotting in the late 1950s.

Lancashire Aircraft Corporation's converted Halifax bomber G-AKEC *Air Voyager*, whilst taking part in the *Daily Express* Hurn to Herne Bay Air Race on 16 September 1950. Behind the Halifax is Airspeed Consul VX587.

Pleasure flying Fox Moth G-AOJH at Manchester Airport in 1959. The original 1938 terminal building is visible in the background.

As previously mentioned, the vast majority of light aircraft in Britain during this period were conversions of military machines. One popular type was the Percival Proctor, which first flew in 1939 and was used by the RAF for communications duties. After the war some 225 Proctors were demobilised and used for club and light charter work. They were also entered for races such as those described above. Some 150 additional Proctor 5s were built post-war at Luton from 1946 onwards.

A contemporary of the Proctor was the Miles Messenger which first flew in 1942 as an Army light liaison aircraft. Post-war the type was civilianised and was much used as a touring and racing aeroplane.

Even when it was photographed at Fair Oaks Aerodrome, Surrey, on 4 September 1958, Tiger Moth G-ACDC was the oldest example on the British civil register. Note the Tiger Club emblem and racing number on the tail, the period Esso petrol pump and the somewhat delapidated control tower.

In 1947 the RAF started releasing its entire inventory of Tiger Moth biplane trainers for sale to private owners. A vast number of these were converted at Croydon by Rollason Aircraft and Engines and during a single month in 1954 no less than 103 were ferried to Croydon for this purpose. A group of Tiger Moth devotees formed the Tiger Club in 1956 and held their first race meeting at Elstree on 1 September using five Tiger Moths owned by the Club founder Mr Norman H. Jones. The Tiger Club was not a conventional flying club as it did not offer basic flying instruction but instead offered experienced pilots the opportunity to convert onto the Tiger Moth and other vintage aircraft that later joined the fleet. Between 1958 and 1960 four standard Tiger Moths were modified by Rollasons at Croydon and became 'Super Tigers', based at the Tiger Club's Redhill aerodrome. The aircraft were named 'The Bishop' (after the Club's Chief Flying Instructor, C. A. Nepean Bishop), 'The Deacon', 'The Archbishop', and 'The Canon'. The Super Tiger was a conversion to competition aerobatics standard and to achieve this the aircraft's fuel tank was moved from the upper wing section to the front cockpit and an inverted fuel system was fitted.

Another Tiger Moth variant was the Thruxton Jackaroo, which was produced by the Wiltshire School of Flying at Thruxton aerodrome. The conversion programme took ten days, cost £600, and transformed the two-seater Tiger Moth into a four-seat touring aircraft. The first Jackaroo flew on 2 March 1957 and twenty such conversions were carried out, several of them for use by the Wiltshire School themselves.

Another military trainer to be the subject of a conversion programme was the Percival Prentice. During 1956 Freddie Laker's Aviation Traders company purchased all 252 RAF-surplus Prentices with the intention of transforming them into civilian touring aircraft. Twenty-eight were converted at Southend and sold to civil owners but the type proved too heavy and expensive to operate for private owners and the vast majority of them were piled up in a corner of Southend Airport and gradually scrapped over the next few years.

One popular touring aircraft that was purpose-built for the civil market was the Miles Gemini, which was the last type built in quantity at Woodley by Miles Aircraft Ltd. The Gemini's high-gloss finish and luxury accommodation made it much in demand for touring and air racing and it was also used by many corporate owners such as Shell-Mex and BP Ltd., whose example G-AMGF was frequently flown by Group Captain Douglas Bader during his time with the company.

Percival Proctor 5 G-AKYB at Biggin Hill, Kent, on 27 July 1959. The period cars in the background would doubtless be collectors' items today.

Large numbers of RAF Chipmunk T Mk.10s were offered for civilian disposal in 1956 following the closure of the Reserve Schools and the move towards all-jet training in the RAF. They were converted to Chipmunk 22s by the Airways Aero Club and used widely by flying clubs and private owners for aerobatic training and competitions.

Auster J/1 Autocrat G-AGOH at Wolverhampton Airport on 9 September 1962. The airfield was closed in 1970.

The contemporary practice of starting light aircraft was by swinging the propellor and this required the presence of a person in the cockpit to operate the throttle, otherwise an embarrassment could occur such as that which befell Auster J-4 G-AJYX at Rearsby on 22 April 1951. The pilot was attempting to start it unaided with the throttle fully open when the engine caught and before he could stop it the Auster accelerated and took off with no-one aboard. It circled for some two hours and reached an altitude of 8,000 feet before finally running out of fuel and being destroyed in the ensuing crash.

In addition to their airline operations Derby Aviation also undertook the civilianisation of military types including a batch of Mosquito P.R.35s, which they prepared at Burnaston in 1955 for Spartan Air Services of Canada. The Mosquitos were ferried to Burnaston from Maintenance Units at Silloth and Shawbury and after conversion they were flown out to Canada via Prestwick.

Derby Aviation operated fully ARB-approved maintenance and repair facilities at Burnaston and at Wolverhampton Airport, which was managed by Don Everall (Aviation) from 1946 until the airfield closed down in 1970. During 1950 Derby Aviation converted over a dozen Miles Geminis to Gypsy Major engine power. Their associate company Air Schools Ltd. operated flying schools at Burnaston and Wolverhampton and in the summer of 1952 they purchased the Elstree Flying Club, thereby bringing their total fleet to twenty aircraft. Derby Aviation acquired an Avro Anson in July 1955 and converted it for geological survey work around the Midlands in the colours of Canadian Aero Services, their partner in this enterprise. In 1957 the survey division was renamed Derby Aero Survey and moved with its fleet of three Austers and the Anson to Elstree. A second Anson later joined the fleet and these aircraft were also used for multi-engined training and for navigational instruction. Eventually the company's name was changed to the London School of Flying, before it was finally sold to Polyfoto Air Taxis.

Another airline which diversified into the aerial survey field was BKS Air Transport who in 1957 set up BKS Air Survey, operating Dakota, Consul and Anson equipment. A Beech 18 was later acquired for this work.

Newly-delivered from the USA, Piper Tri-Pacer 160 G-APVA was photographed at Barton Airfield, Manchester on 8 August 1959.

An aviation activity almost unique to the 1950s was aerial advertising. In September 1952 Air Ads Ltd. was started at Southend by Mr L. C. Marmol and a Miles Aerovan was purchased, its large slab sides being fitted with neon tubes for displaying illuminated messages at night. During the daytime this aircraft was used for banner towing and it also carried fish and fish products from the Continent into the UK. A second aircraft was acquired in 1955 but by the end of 1956 both machines had been written off whilst carrying out this rather hazardous night flying work and the company's operations were suspended.

In 1947 the construction company Sir Robert McAlpine & Sons Ltd. set up an aviation division at Fair Oaks airfield in Surrey to transport their executives around Britain and the Continent. By the time they relocated their operations base to Luton Airport ten years later their fleet consisted of a Rapide, a Gemini and a Lockheed 12. At Luton McAlpines acquired their own hangar, staffed by an aircraft maintenance division whose duties included laying out flare-paths for night landings by their aircraft. The relaxation of import restrictions at the end of the 1950s permitted the influx of American and European aircraft types such as the Piper Apache and McAlpines purchased one of these in 1958. This was followed in April 1959 by the first production example of the Italian Piaggio P.166. McAlpines were appointed British distributor of this twin-engined executive aircraft and over the next few years they operated them on behalf of many UK corporate owners such as the Stanley Estate and Stud Company, the Marley Tile Company, John Laing and Co., and United Steel. The Piaggio had a useful short-field performance and could carry seven passengers in and out of small grass airfields such as Netherthorpe and Chepstow Racecourse. In 1961 the company entered the air taxi business with the formation of McAlpine Aviation at Luton Airport. The initial air taxi fleet comprised two four-seat Cessna 310s, and from 1964 the Piaggio P.166 also became available for hire. McAlpines became the European agency for the Riley conversion of the De Havilland Dove in July 1964. Many conversions were sold and the company retained two for use on their own charter operations. In 1965 McAlpines set up a complete maintenance organisation for the HS-125 executive jet at Luton Airport. Their first customer was Air Gregory, who were the first British air taxi company to operate the type.

On 13 July 1959 an air race with a difference took place. This was the *Daily Mail* London-Paris Air Race, held to commemorate the 50th anniversary of Louis Bleriot's Channel crossing. A prize of £5,000 was offered for the fastest journey from Marble Arch in London to the Arc De Triomphe in Paris, using any combination of surface and air transportation. The contest ran for eleven days and many types of aircraft were used, ranging from small light aircraft to modern military jets. The fastest overall time was achieved by Squadron Leader Charles Maugham, C.O. of 65 Squadron at Duxford who used a motor cycle, Bristol Sycamore helicopter, Hawker Hunter T. Mk.7, another Sycamore and another motor-cycle to win on behalf of the RAF in a total time of 40 minutes 44 seconds. Among the other entrants was the BEA-line syndicate entered by BEA. This was a group of businessmen (and one business-lady!) who travelled complete with bowler hats and umbrellas and used 'public transport' throughout. From Marble Arch they travelled to Paddington Station in a hired London Transport bus, then took the 'tube' to RAF Northolt where they boarded BEA Comet 4B G-APMA for a twenty-seven minute flight to Le Bourget Airport, Paris. From there they took a taxi to the Arc De Triomphe, the taxi driver completing this leg of the journey in thirteen minutes!

After an absence of twenty-two years the London to Cardiff Air Race was revived on 3 June 1960. Forty-one starters flew the course from White Waltham aerodrome to Rhoose Airport, Cardiff and in fifth place, competing in her first air race, was Miss Sheila Scott in her silver and blue Thruxton Jackaroo G-APAM 'Myth', at an average speed of 115.25mph. Sheila Scott was to earn great public acclaim in the late 1960s for her round the world solo record-breaking flights but she began in a more modest fashion on 19 May 1965 by setting up nine new European city centre-to-city centre records on the same day. Taking off from Northolt in her Piper Commanche 400 N8515P 'Myth Sunpip', she flew London-The Hague-London-Brussels-London-Paris-London without landing to establish the new records. On the following day she flew non-stop London-Belfast-London-Dublin-London to set up six more records. In each of these two sessions record timings were achieved for both the outward and return legs of each city pair and for the round-trip journey times.

In May 1963 Mr Ted Drewery and Squadron Leader 'Jock' Maitland organised the very first Biggin Hill Air Fair. At these shows great emphasis was placed on providing opportunities for people who had not flown before to inspect and fly in the types of airliner used on holiday charter flights, and in addition to pleasure flights in light aircraft joy-rides were also offered in such types as the Avro 748 and the Caravelle. At the 1964 Air Fair the author was among those privileged to fly around the Biggin Hill circuit aboard Air Links Hermes 4 G-ALDA, the last commercially-operated Hermes in the world.

Auster 5 G-ANDU, used by Skyneon Ltd for night advertising flights is seen in the hangar at Manchester (Ringway) on 12 January 1954. Beneath the wings can be seen the framework supporting the neon tubes used to display illuminated slogans.

An early 1960s line-up of McAlpine Aviation aircraft and personnel outside their hangar at Luton Airport. The aircraft on view comprise two Piaggio P.166s, two Rapides, a Cessna 310 and a Lockheed 12.

A Miles Aerovan, operated by Meridian Airmaps on photo survey flights, is seen here outside the Municipal Flying School hangar at Woolsington Airport, Newcastle, in the early 1950s.

The sole completed Bristol Brabazon, which first flew on 4 September 1949. The people on the steps show just how large this aircraft was for its time.

Chapter 15

The Way Things Might Have Been

During the 1950s and the years immediately preceding them three British aircraft projects were commenced which were destined not to reach production status despite protracted testing. Had they done so however they may well have altered considerably the development of commercial aviation in Britain.

The first of these to emerge was the BRISTOL BRABAZON. The Brabazon was built in response to one of the proposals of the 1943 Brabazon Committee which had been set up while the war was still in progress to determine the fleet requirements of the post-war airline industry. The aircraft was conceived as a long-range trans-Atlantic landplane capable of carrying 100 passengers from London to New York non-stop. This ability to operate across the Atlantic without refuelling would have conferred much prestige on the airline concerned (BOAC, naturally) and would have made possible a much more reliable and regular service, free of weather considerations at en route airfields.

The Brabazon was the most ambitious airliner project attempted by the British aircraft industry up to that time and the Bristol Aeroplane Company was selected as the constructor because of their design experience with a long-range strategic bomber project which had been cancelled in 1942. Another point in their favour was that the company was already building the engine chosen to power the Brabazon, the Bristol Centaurus radial piston engine. Eight of these engines were to be coupled in pairs, with each pair driving two three-bladed contra-rotating propellors. These engines were contained within the thickness of the giant wings, whose 230 feet span was considerably greater than that of today's Boeing 747s. The 177 feet long fuselage was originally to have been of 'double-bubble' construction but this would have created too much drag for the engines then available and so a single-deck arrangement seating ninety-six day passengers or fifty-two in sleeping berths was decided upon. At the operating altitude of 20,000 feet and a cruising speed of 250mph the range was estimated to be in excess of 5,000 miles. A projected development, the Brabazon II, would have been fitted with Bristol Proteus turbo-prop engines.

BOAC decreed that eighteen hours was the longest flight duration that their passengers could be expected to tolerate without a break and that each of them should have at least 200 cubic feet of cabin space, or 270 cubic feet in a luxury configuration.

Construction began at Filton in 1947 in the face of considerable local opposition brought about by the closure of a newly-completed dual carriageway road and the demolition of part of a village in order to build the new and lengthy runway necessary for the test flying. A special three-bay eight acre assembly hall was also erected specifically for the Brabazon project during the winter of 1947/8. The prototype aircraft G-AGPW was rolled out on 6 January 1949 as an unfurnished test-bed but it was not until 4 September that it made its maiden flight in the hands of Bristol Chief Test Pilot Bill Pegg. The trouble-free first flight lasted twenty-five minutes and the Brabazon proved to be smooth and comfortable to fly in, the eighty-seven-ton aircraft lifting off the runway at 87mph after a take-off run of only 1500 feet. After a second flight three days later the Brabazon was displayed at the 1949 Farnborough Air Show, fitted out with thirty BOAC reclining seats for demonstration purposes.

In BOAC service the Brabazon would have carried ninety-four passengers and fourteen crew members and its direct operating cost was estimated at £400 per flying hour.

The aircraft then continued its test programme which was mainly concerned with various engine installations, and paid visits to London Airport, where it was inspected by the Minister of Supply and other officials and Prestwick where it attracted a crowd of over 3,000 spectators on 28 August 1951.

In the meantime construction of the second prototype was also proceeding and by the end of 1951 it had reached the final assembly stage. By 1952 however it was becoming apparent that the sales prospects for the Brabazon were very poor, with airlines all over the world ordering the more readily available modern American types. In February 1952 the government ordered the temporary suspension of work on the Brabazon II project, pending more favourable sales conditions. This did not come as too much of a blow to Bristols, who were by then well into production of the Britannia and needed the hangar space. On 9 July 1953 the cancellation of the entire Brabazon programme was announced and on 17 August Bristols were authorised to abandon the project. The Brabazon I prototype had been taken into the air for the last time on 20 September 1952 and it was scrapped at Filton in October 1953 along with the completed components of the second aircraft, having amassed a total of 382 hours 15 minutes flying time. It was the largest landplane ever built in Britain and had cost some £3 million at the time of its cancellation. The experience gained did prove useful however in the Britannia and Concorde programmes.

In 1946 the Ministry of Supply authorised the Saunders-Roe Company to proceed with the construction of three S.R. 45 PRINCESS flying boats for use by BOAC.

These giant machines were to be the largest flying-boats ever built, with a wingspan of 219 feet 6 inches and a fuselage length of 148 feet. Ten Bristol Proteus turbo-prop engines were to power the aircraft, eight of them paired in the four inner nacelles and the other two mounted singly outboard. These engines were to give the aircraft a still-air range of 5,500 miles and a cruising speed of 360mph, and the Princess was to be ten tons heavier than even the mighty Brabazon I which preceded it.

The gigantic pressurised hull was divided into two decks on which BOAC planned to carry 105 passengers in Tourist and First Class cabins and to provide powder rooms, bunks and a connecting spiral staircase.

Problems with the pressurisation of the hull, which was the largest pressurised structure built up to that time, delayed the maiden flight until late in 1952. By this time BOAC had ceased operating flying-boats completely but they did carry out a survey of their maintenance base at Hythe to determine what alterations would be necessary to accommodate the Princesses. Shortly afterwards however they announced that they were no longer interested in the Princess programme.

After much confusion at government level over the future of the aircraft, including a proposal for the RAF to operate them as 200-seat strategic troop carriers, it was announced that only the first prototype would be completed and flown and that the almost fully-assembled second machine and parts for the third would be mothballed pending the development of more powerful engines.

The mighty Saunders-Roe Princess flying-boat in flight. G-ALUN was demonstrated at the 1952 and 1953 Farnborough Air Shows before its development was abandoned.

The Princess prototype G-ALUN was launched on 20 August 1952 and two days later, after waiting for the wash from the liner RMS *Mauretania* to subside, the aircraft became airborne after a twenty-five-second take-off run on its maiden flight. The Chairman of BOAC, Sir Miles Thomas, flew alongside the Princess in a BOAC Dove during the first flight, and the prototype was displayed at the 1952 and 1953 Farnborough Air Shows, but it was eventually beached and cocooned at Calshot alongside the components of the other two examples in 1954. The cost of the Princess programme had escalated from a projected £2,800,000 in 1946 to almost £11 million by 1951. All three machines were eventually scrapped in 1967.

The first serious attempt at producing a rotary-winged airliner for scheduled services between city centres was the FAIREY ROTODYNE.

The original 1947 proposal was for a fifteen-seat machine but by 1951 this had been revised to meet a BEA 'BEAline-Bus' specification for a thirty-five to forty-seater powered by two Napier Eland turbo-props. A contract was awarded to Fairey Aviation by the Ministry of Supply on 12 June 1953 for a single prototype and the military serial XE521 was allocated to reflect the aircraft's additional potential as a battlefield support transport.

When completed the Rotodyne had a capacious box-like fuselage, a large single rotor pylon and twin tail fins. The Napier Eland engines were slung under substantial stub wings and provided forward propulsion whilst vertical lift was generated by the four-bladed rotor which was driven by compressed air bled from the main engines and forced out through pressure jets at the tip of each blade.

The Rotodyne was assembled at Hayes and Stockport and made its first untethered flight on 6 November 1957, the first transitions between vertical and horizontal flight following during 1958. The normal flight profile consisted of a vertical ascent to 1,000 feet and transition to forward flight at speeds of around 185mph. The Eland engines and the stub wings contributed over half of the total lift necessary and enabled high speeds to be achieved. On 5 January 1959 Rotodyne established a new 100km closed-circuit record for convertiplanes of 190.9mph.

The prototype took part in the 1958 and 1959 Farnborough Air Shows and the 1959 Paris Air Show and much interest was initially shown by airlines. A manufacturing licence for the USA was taken out by the Kaman Aircraft Corporation and prospective operators included Okanagan Helicopters of Canada, New York Airways, Japan Air Lines, BEA and the US Army, with talk of a possible order for 200 examples. The main drawback to commercial operation though, and a problem that was never satisfactorily solved, was the almost unbearable level of noise from the rotor-tip pressure jets. Some progress was made but the Rotodyne was still intolerably noisy, especially on the ground.

In 1960 the helicopter division of Faireys was forced by the government into a merger with Westlands. The military version of the Rotodyne was dropped on cost grounds and BEA consequently decided that they could not continue with their order as the sole customer. The project was cancelled on

The prototype Fairey Rotodyne in flight, showing its airliner-type fuselage and the troublesome blade-tip pressure-jets.

26 February 1962. Eventually on 8 December 1964 the airframe was disposed of to the famous aircraft scrap merchants R.J. Coley Ltd., but several large components were rescued and preserved at Weston-super-Mare by the British Rotorcraft Museum.

Bibliography

The following publications have proved invaluable as sources of reference in the compilation of this book, and are recommended for further reading:

Diamonds in the Sky, Kenneth Hudson and Julian Pettifer (The Bodley Head and BBC Publications 1979)

British Transport Since 1914, Derek H. Aldcroft (David and Charles 1975)

British Flying Boats and Amphibians 1909–1952, G. R. Duval (Putnams 1966)

Travel Trade Gazette – reprints of various 1953 editions

High Risk – The Politics Of The Air, Adam Thomson (Sidgwick & Jackson 1990)

The Story of Aberdeen Airport, James D. Ferguson (Scottish Airports 1984)

Prestwick Airport Golden Jubilee 1935–1985, Jim Ewart (Scottish Airports 1985)

British Independent Airlines Since 1946, A. C. Merton-Jones (LAAS International & MAS 1976)

The Water Jump, David Beaty (Secker & Warburg 1976)

Croydon to Concorde, Captain R. E. Gilman (John Murray Ltd 1980)

British Research and Development Aircraft, Ray Sturtivant (Haynes Publishing Group 1990)

The Tiger Moth Story, Stuart McKay (Airlife Publishing 1987)

British Civil Aircraft Since 1919, A. J. Jackson (Putnams 1974)

The Lockheed Constellation, M. J. Hardy (David and Charles 1973)

Vickers Viscount 700, P. St John Turner (Airline Publications and Sales 1973)

An Illustrated History of Liverpool Airport, P. H. Butler (Merseyside Aviation Society 1983)

Golden Gatwick – 50 Years of Aviation, John King and Geoffrey Tait (Royal Aeronautical Society Gatwick Branch and BAA 1980)

Sky Tramps, P. Jackson (Souvenir Press 1965)

The Annals of British and Commonwealth Air Transport, John Stroud (Putnams)

Flying to the Sun, Geoffrey Cuthbert (Hodder & Stoughton 1987)

Rebels and Reformers of the Airways, R. E. G. Davies (Airlife Publishing 1987)

Pictorial History of Pan American World Airways, P. St John Turner (Ian Allan Ltd 1973)

British Racing and Record-Breaking Aircraft, Peter Lewis (Putnams 1970)

BEA Chronology (BEA Public Relations 1972)

Wings Across the World – An Illustrated History of British Airways, Harald Penrose (Cassell Ltd 1980)

First and Foremost – 50 Years of Manchester's Civic Airports, R. A. Scholefield and S. D. McDonald (Manchester International Airport Authority 1978)

Southampton/Eastleigh Airport, David Hatchard (Kingfisher Publications 1990)

Major Airliner Types

1950-1965

AIRSPEED A.S.57 AMBASSADOR Medium range pressurised airliner. High wing, triple fins. Two Bristol Centaurus piston engines. Capacity up to fifty five passengers. Twenty aircraft operated by BEA on major European routes until replaced by Viscounts in 1958. Then used extensively by independent airlines such as Dan-Air and BKS Air Transport on scheduled services and inclusive-tour charters. Also used by Shell as executive aircraft, and as engine test-bed.

AIRSPEED A.S. 65 CONSUL Short range light transport based on wartime Oxford trainer. Low wing, single fin. Two Armstrong Siddeley Cheetah piston engines. Capacity up to six passengers. More than 150 produced. Used by charter airlines such as Morton Air Services from 1946 onwards.

AVIATION TRADERS ATL-98 CARVAIR Medium range unpressurised car-ferry conversion of Douglas DC-4, incorporating new nose section and tail fin. Low wing, single fin. Flight deck relocated above main cabin to allow cars to be driven in through nose doors. Four Pratt and Whitney Twin Wasp piston engines. Capacity for up to five cars and twenty-two passengers. Used by Channel Air Bridge, British United Air Ferries and Aer Lingus from 1962 onwards.

AVRO ANSON Short range light transport. Anson I was wartime trainer adapted for civil use. Avro 19 was postwar civil version. Low wing, single fin. Two Armstrong Siddeley Cheetah piston engines. Capacity up to eight passengers or cargo. Used by many small charter companies. In production until 1952.

AVRO 685 YORK Medium range unpressurised cargo or passenger transport. Developed from wartime Lancaster bomber, using original wings, engines, undercarriage and tail unit married to new transport fuselage. High wing, triple fins. Four Rolls-Royce Merlin piston engines. Operated by BOAC in immediate post-war years, then used by independent airlines such as Dan-Air and Skyways for trooping and cargo flights.

AVRO 748 Short range pressurised airliner, designed as 'Dakota-replacement'. Low wing, single fin. Two Rolls-Royce Dart turbo-prop engines. Capacity up to fifty-eight passengers. First flew 1960. Initial UK operator Skyways Coach-Air. Also used by BKS Air Transport for scheduled services.

BAC One-Eleven Short-medium range pressurised jet airliner. Low wing, single fin. Two rear-mounted Rolls-Royce Spey turbo-fan engines. Capacity up to seventy-nine passengers (srs 200). First short-haul jet airliner to enter service. Intended as jet successor to Viscount. Inaugural airline service, with British United Airways, on 9 April 1965.

Boeing 377 Stratocruiser Long range pressurised airliner. Developed from wartime B-29 bomber, with original wings, undercarriage and tail unit, but with new 'double-bubble' airliner fuselage. Low wing, single fin. Four Pratt and Whitney Wasp Major piston engines. Used on luxury trans-Atlantic sleeper services by BOAC and Pan American Airways from 1949. Later leased out to Nigeria Airways and Ghana Airways for West African services until retirement in 1959.

Boeing 707 Long range pressurised jet airliner based on contemporary KC-135 tanker/military transport. Low wing, single fin. Four Pratt and Whitney JT3C (initial versions) or Rolls-Royce Conway turbo-jet engines. Capacity up to 189 passengers or cargo. Operated by Pan American Airways, BOAC and TWA on trans-Atlantic routes and by many other national carriers on long-haul flights into the UK.

Bristol 170 Short range unpressurised cargo and passenger transport. High wing, single fin. Two Bristol Hercules piston engines. All-passenger variant known as Bristol Wayfarer. Operated from 1948 onwards by Silver City Airways, Dan-Air, Air Charter Ltd. and others. Developed into Mk 32 Superfreighter, designed specifically for car-ferry operations. Capacity 3 cars plus up to 20 passengers or all-cargo.

Bristol 175 Britannia Long range pressurised airliner. Low wing, single fin. Four Bristol Proteus turbo-prop engines. Capacity up to 139 passengers or cargo. Initial srs 100 version used by BOAC on routes to Africa and Far East from 1957. Developed srs 300 variant operated by BOAC on trans-Atlantic services. After retirement from BOAC service both versions widely used by Britannia Airways, BKS Air Transport and British Eagle.

Canadair C-4 Argonaut (and North Star) Long-range pressurised airliner. Basically a pressurised development of the Douglas DC-4. Low wing, single fin. Four Rolls-Royce Merlin piston engines. Capacity up to fifty-four passengers (BOAC service). In Trans-Canada Air Lines service was known as North Star and used on Canada-UK services until mid-1950s. BOAC version was Argonaut. Over twenty examples operated on routes to Africa and Far East. Both variants later used on charter flights by independents such as Overseas Aviation and Derby Airways.

Convair 240/340/440 Series Family of short-medium range pressurised airliners. Low wing, single fin. Two Pratt and Whitney Double Wasp piston engines. Capacity forty to fifty-two passengers. Used extensively on European routes from early 1950s by many airlines such as KLM, SABENA, Iberia and Swissair but not operated commercially by British airlines.

DE HAVILLAND DH89A RAPIDE Short range unpressurised feeder-liner. Biplane, single fin. Two De Havilland Gypsy Queen piston engines. Capacity six to eight passengers. Used in large numbers in early 1950s by BEA on Scottish, Channel Island and Scilly Isles routes, then acquired by many small carriers for scheduled and charter operations.

DE HAVILLAND DH104 DOVE Short range unpressurised feeder-liner. Intended as successor to Rapide. First successful post-war British airliner design. Low wing, single fin. Two De Havilland Gypsy Queen piston engines. Capacity up to eight passengers. Used widely by Morton Air Services and many other small airlines and corporate owners.

DE HAVILLAND DH114 HERON Short range unpressurised airliner development of smaller Dove aircraft. Low wing, single fin. Four De Havilland Gypsy Queen piston engines. Capacity up to seventeen passengers. Operated on BEA Scottish routes and air ambulance services and by Jersey Airlines and other airlines and corporate owners.

DE HAVILLAND DH106 COMET Medium and long range pressurised jet airliner. Low wing, single fin. Initial srs 1 version was the first jet airliner to enter service and was used to open BOAC jet schedule to South Africa in 1952. Four Rolls-Royce Ghost jet engines. Withdrawn from use following in-flight structural failures in 1954. Developed Comet 4 introduced by BOAC on first trans-Atlantic jet services in 1958. Four Rolls-Royce Avon jet engines. Medium range Comet 4B used by BEA on European routes from 1960. Capacity up to 102 passengers (srs 4B).

DE HAVILLAND DH121 TRIDENT Medium range pressurised jet airliner. Low wing, single fin. Three rear-mounted Rolls-Royce Spey turbo-fan engines. Capacity up to 103 passengers. Commenced full scheduled operations with BEA on 1 April 1964.

DOUGLAS DAKOTA Short range unpressurised airliner. World's most widely used transport aircraft. Most civil aircraft were conversions of wartime C-47 military transports. Low wing, single fin. Two Pratt and Whitney Twin Wasp piston engines. Capacity up to thirty-six passengers or cargo. Used by BEA and most European airlines for scheduled services, then acquired by many independent operators for scheduled and charter work.

DOUGLAS DC-4 Medium range unpressurised airliner. Civilian conversion of C-54 military transport. Low wing, single fin. Four Pratt and Whitney Twin Wasp piston engines. Capacity up to 86 passengers or cargo. Used on first trans-Atlantic services, then operated on European scheduled services and charter flights.

DOUGLAS DC-6 Medium range pressurised airliner. Development of earlier DC-4. Low wing, single fin. Four Pratt and Whitney Double Wasp piston engines. Capacity up to 102 passengers or cargo. Developments included DC-6A cargo version and refined DC-6B passenger version. Used by Pan American Airways to pioneer trans-Atlantic Tourist Class services and by many European scheduled carriers and charter operators.

DOUGLAS DC-7 Long range pressurised airliner. Further development of DC-4 and DC-6 series. Low wing, single fin. Four Wright Turbo Compound piston engines. Capacity up to 105 passengers or cargo. Developed DC-7B used by Pan American on trans-Atlantic routes and by South African Airways Johannesburg-London. Ultimate version the DC-7C was first airliner capable of non-stop trans-Atlantic service in both directions and was operated by BOAC and Pan American.

DOUGLAS DC-8 (srs 10 to 50) Long range pressurised jet airliner. Contemporary of Boeing 707. Low wing, single fin. Four Pratt and Whitney JT3D or Rolls-Royce Conway turbo-jets. Capacity up to 189 passengers or cargo. Used by Trans-Canada Air Lines and Pan American Airways for trans-Atlantic services into UK.

FOKKER F-27 FRIENDSHIP Short range pressurised airliner. Designed as 'Dakota replacement'. High wing, single fin. Two Rolls-Royce Dart turbo-prop engines. Capacity up to forty-eight passengers. First European operator was Aer Lingus who used the type extensively on Ireland-UK services from 1958.

HANDLEY PAGE H.P.81 HERMES Medium range pressurised airliner. Low wing, single fin. Four Bristol Hercules piston engines. Capacity up to seventy-four passengers. Used by BOAC on African routes 1950-1954, then operated by independent airlines such as Skyways and Airwork for trooping and inclusive-tour charters.

HANDLEY PAGE HPR7 HERALD Short range pressurised airliner. Designed as 'Dakota replacement'. High wing, single fin. Two Rolls-Royce Dart turbo-prop engines. Capacity up to fifty-six passengers. Used by BEA on Scottish internal routes from 1959 and by Jersey Airlines on extensive Channel Islands route network from 1962.

LOCKHEED L-049 and L-749 CONSTELLATION Long range pressurised airliner. Low wing, triple fins. Four Wright Cyclone piston engines. Capacity up to eighty-one passengers or cargo. Used by Pan American Airways, TWA and BOAC to open trans-Atlantic routes from 1946. Later used by Skyways, Euravia and ACE Freighters for inclusive-tour and cargo charters.

LOCKHEED L-1049 SUPER CONSTELLATION Long range pressurised airliner. Development of original Constellation design. Low wing, triple fins. Four Wright Turbo-Compound piston engines. Capacity up to ninety-nine passengers or cargo. Operated on trans-Atlantic routes into London by TWA and Trans-Canada Air Lines, and on Far East routes by QANTAS and Air India.

LOCKHEED L-1649 STARLINER Long range pressurised airliner. Ultimate development of Constellation series. Low wing, triple fins. Four Wright Turbo-Compound piston engines. Capacity up to ninety-nine passengers. Had non-stop trans-Atlantic capability and used by TWA on USA-London services but quickly rendered obsolescent by Boeing 707.

MILES M.57 AEROVAN Short range unpressurised passenger transport/ freighter. High wing, triple fins. Two Blackburn Cirrus Major piston engines. Capacity up to nine passengers or cargo, loaded through clam-shell doors at rear. Used by many small UK operators from 1946.

SHORT S.45 SOLENT Medium range unpressurised flying-boat. High wing, single fin. Four Bristol Hercules piston engines. Capacity up to thirty-six passengers. Used by BOAC on African routes until 1950 and by Aquila Airways on tourist services to Madeira from 1948 to 1958.

SUD AVIATION SE210 CARAVELLE Medium range pressurised jet airliner. Low wing, single fin. Two rear-mounted Rolls-Royce Avon turbo-jets. Capacity up to ninety-nine passengers. Used extensively on routes into London from 1959 by most European national carriers except Lufthansa and BEA.

TUPOLEV TU-104 Medium range pressurised jet airliner. Based on TU-16 jet bomber. Low wing, single fin. Two Mikulin turbo-jet engines. Capacity up to 100 passengers (TU-104B). Operated from USSR to London by Aeroflot from 1958. First Aeroflot jet airliner.

VICKERS VIKING Short-medium range unpressurised airliner. Based on wartime Wellington bomber, with original wings and engines but with new transport fuselage. Low wing, single fin. Two Bristol Hercules piston engines. Capacity up to thirty-six passengers. Used extensively by BEA on European network 1946-1954. Large numbers of ex-BEA machines acquired for charter work by most British independent airlines.

VICKERS VISCOUNT Medium range pressurised airliner. World's first turbo-prop airliner. Low wing, single fin. Four Rolls-Royce Dart turbo-prop engines. Capacity up to seventy-one passengers (srs 800). Entered BEA service in 1953 and used extensively on European network. Also operated into UK by many European national carriers and used for charter work by UK independent airlines.

VICKERS VANGUARD Medium range pressurised airliner. Intended as high-capacity successor to Viscount. Low wing, single fin. Four Rolls-Royce Tyne turbo-prop engines. Capacity up to 139 passengers. Entered regular service with BEA in 1961.

VICKERS VC-10 Long range pressurised jet airliner. Low wing, single fin. Four rear-mounted Rolls-Royce Conway turbo-fan engines. Capacity up to 187 passengers (Super VC-10). Standard VC-10 operated by BOAC on African and Far East routes from April 1964. Developed Super VC-10 for trans-Atlantic operations entered BOAC service in April 1965.

Index

Aberdeen (Dyce) Airport   63, 64, 66
ACE Freighters   117
Aer Lingus   9, 11, 21, 62, 63, 65, 72, 75, 76, 78, 81, 82, 84, 85, 86, 112, 115, 120, 123
Aeroflot   36, 39
Aerolineas Argentinas   39
Aero Commander srs 500   90
Aerovan, Miles   132, 133, 139, 155
Air Ads Ltd   139
Air Ceylon   36
Air Charter Ltd   56, 97, 102, 104, 110, 112, 117
Air Couriers Ltd   58
Air Ferry   125
Air France   33, 39, 40, 79, 82, 107
Air Gregory   139
Air Kruise   116, 120
Air Links   56, 117, 125, 140
Air Ministry   99, 100, 102, 104, 115, 117
Air Navigation and Trading   131
Air Safaris (and African Air Safaris)   56, 68, 70, 83, 90, 121, 122
Air Transport Licencing Board   61
Airviews Ltd   80, 82
Airways Corporation Act of 1949   14
Airwork Ltd   14, 23, 47, 56, 61, 95, 97, 99, 100
Aldermaston Airfield   114
Alderney Airport   55, 90, 91
Ambassador, Airspeed (and 'Elizabethan' class)   22, 27, 29, 31, 36, 37, 65, 68, 70, 72, 73, 77, 79, 83, 116, 117, 121, 124, 129, 151
American Overseas Airlines   11, 43
Anson, Avro (and Avro 19)   11, 12, 24, 78, 115, 138, 151
Apache, Piper   139
Aquila Airways   13, 18, 19, 115
Argonaut, Canadair   14, 28, 30, 31, 32, 39, 56, 97, 120, 124, 125, 152
Argosy, Armstrong Whitworth   40
Associated Airways Joint Committee (AAJC)   9, 11, 12
Auster (various models)   11, 132, 133, 137, 138
Austrian Airlines   82
Autair   37, 73, 124
Aviation Traders   14, 102, 113, 136
Avro 748   72, 106, 140, 151

Bamberg, Harold   13, 63, 75, 114, 119
Barra Airfield   62
BEA Associate Agreements   12, 23, 61, 75, 85, 93
BEA Helicopters   87
Beech 18   138
Belfast Airport (Nutts Corner and Aldergrove)   14, 63, 64, 65, 68, 70, 71, 72, 77, 79, 83, 86, 120
Bell 47   36, 55
Benbecula Airport   24
Berlin Airlift   12, 13, 14, 18, 99
Biggin Hill Air Fair   140
Birkdale Sands Aerodrome, Southport   130
Birmingham (Elmdon) Airport   39, 62, 65, 70, 77, 79, 80, 83, 84, 90, 120, 121, 124
Birmingham (Haymills Rotorstation)   83
BKS Air Transport (and BKS Aerocharter)   37, 65, 67, 68, 70, 71, 72, 112, 114, 116, 119, 138
Blackbushe Airport   14, 91, 95, 100, 102, 104, 113, 115, 116, 119, 120, 121
Blackpool (Squires Gate) Airport   14, 72, 73, 74, 90, 105, 123, 131
Boeing 707   36, 37, 39, 49, 50, 51, 52, 152
Bond Air Services   14
Bournemouth (Hurn) Airport   10, 11, 68, 70, 72, 74, 83, 86, 90, 91, 92, 110, 121, 133
Bovingdon Airport   23, 68, 95, 97, 99, 101, 113, 114
Brabazon, Bristol   143, 144, 145
Brabazon Committee 1943   143
Brawdy Airfield   24
Bristol 170 Freighter (and Superfreighter and Wayfarer)   65, 72, 73, 74, 75, 93, 107, 109, 110, 111, 112, 115, 116, 117, 120, 121
Bristol 171 Sycamore   36, 55, 83, 90, 139
Bristol Airport (Whitchurch and Lulsgate)   23, 63, 77, 81, 85, 86, 87, 90, 91, 112, 124, 125
Britannia, Bristol   36, 39, 48, 49, 50, 51, 52, 57, 63, 65, 70, 77, 97, 104, 117, 123, 124, 126, 144, 152
Britannia Airways   122, 123, 124
Britavia   61, 102, 107, 116
British Eagle International Airlines   63, 65, 75, 77, 84, 117, 119

British European Airways (BEA)   9, 11, 12, 21, 22, 23, 27, 28, 29, 31, 32, 33, 34, 35, 36, 37, 39, 40, 41, 55, 56, 57, 61, 62, 63, 64, 65, 66, 68, 72, 74, 75, 76, 77, 78, 79, 80, 81, 82, 83, 85, 86, 87, 90, 91, 93, 107, 119, 120, 121, 140, 146
British Midland Airways   85
British Overseas Airways Corporation (BOAC)   9, 10, 11, 12, 14, 17, 18, 27, 28, 29, 30, 31, 32, 33, 34, 36, 37, 39, 40, 41, 43, 45, 46, 47, 48, 49, 50, 52, 58, 61, 63, 65, 95, 97, 100, 102, 113, 114, 116, 117, 120, 123, 143, 144, 145, 146
British South American Airways Corporation (BSAAC)   9, 10, 14, 113
British United Air Ferries   112
British United Airways (including BUA(CI))   34, 56, 57, 58, 65, 73, 74, 90, 91, 93, 97, 103, 104, 107, 112, 120, 126
British Westpoint Airlines   88, 89
Burtonwood Airfield   22, 64

Caledonian Airways   58, 109, 126
Cambrian Airways (and Cambrian Air Services)   12, 24, 63, 75, 76, 77, 81, 85, 86, 87, 90, 91, 116, 125, 132
Cambridge Airport   117, 123
Campbeltown Airport   63
Capitol Airways   58
Caravelle, Sud Est   39, 63, 77, 82, 140, 155
Cardiff Airport (Pengam Moors and Rhoose)   12, 23, 63, 74, 75, 77, 81, 85, 86, 87, 88, 90, 91, 123, 124, 125, 140
Carlisle Airport   72, 74
Carvair, Aviation Traders   112, 151
Castle Kennedy Aerodrome   110
Central African Airways   95, 97
Cessna 310   139
Channel Air Bridge   112
Channel Airways   93, 120, 125
Chipmunk, De Havilland Canada   137
Chrisair   131
Cie Air Transport   107, 112
Civil Aviation Act of 1946   11
Civil Aviation (Licencing) Act of 1960   61
CL-44, Canadair   52
Comet, De Havilland   15, 30, 31, 32, 33, 36, 39, 41, 49, 50, 64, 140, 153
Commanche, Piper   140
Constellation, Lockheed   9, 11, 12, 17, 27, 30, 33, 36, 37, 43, 44, 45, 96, 116, 117, 123, 154
Consul, Airspeed   11, 23, 68, 70, 133, 138, 151
Convair 240/340/440 srs   31, 34, 80, 82, 152
Coventry (Bagington) Airport   83, 91, 112, 132

Crewsair   102, 113, 114
Croydon Airport   11, 21, 23, 24, 29, 56, 91, 120, 129, 135
Cunard Eagle Airways   97, 117

Daily Express International Air Race   133
Daily Mail London-Paris Air Race   139
Dakota, Douglas C-47   11, 13, 14, 21, 22, 23, 24, 36, 39, 40, 56, 57, 61, 62, 63, 64, 65, 66, 67, 68, 71, 72, 73, 74, 75, 76, 77, 79, 80, 81, 83, 84, 85, 86, 87, 89, 90, 91, 93, 100, 105, 106, 113, 116, 119, 120, 121, 124, 138, 153
Dan-Air Services   37, 77, 86, 91, 107, 115, 116, 119, 121
DC-4, Douglas   11, 33, 47, 50, 57, 76, 77, 79, 80, 93, 102, 117, 119, 125, 153
DC-6, Douglas   14, 31, 33, 34, 39, 45, 46, 47, 48, 50, 52, 57, 82, 104, 117, 121, 126, 153
DC-7, Douglas   33, 48, 49, 50, 52, 58, 154
DC-8, Douglas   39, 50, 52, 154
Derby Airways (and Derby Aviation)   56, 72, 84, 85, 116, 124, 137, 138
Derby (Burnaston) Airport   84, 85, 116, 124, 137, 138
Don Everall Aviation   83, 138
Dove, De Havilland   23, 24, 56, 75, 77, 82, 86, 93, 139, 146
Dragon Airways   68, 72, 75, 76
Dragon, De Havilland   131

Eagle Airways (and Eagle Aviation)   13, 14, 23, 75, 81, 82, 99, 100, 101, 102, 104, 113, 114, 116, 117, 119, 120
East African Airways   97
East Anglian Flying Services   93
East Midlands Airport   85, 107
Edinburgh (Turnhouse) Airport   21, 62, 63, 64, 65, 66, 68, 83
El Al Israel Airlines   44, 123
Electra, Lockheed L-188   36
Euravia   96, 106, 122, 123, 124
Exeter Airport   23, 72, 82, 83, 88, 89, 91

F-27, Fokker   63, 76, 82, 154
Fair Oaks Airfield   139
Falcon Airways   122
Federated Air Transport   115
Finglands Aviation   78
Flight Refuelling Ltd   13
Fox Moth, De Havilland   130

Gatwick Airport   11, 14, 24, 55, 56, 57, 58, 65, 72, 73, 90, 91, 103, 104, 107, 109, 117, 120, 121, 123, 125, 126
Gemini, Miles   24, 133, 136, 138, 139

Giro Aviation 130
Glasgow Airport (Renfrew and Abbotsinch)
  12, 50, 61, 62, 63, 64, 65, 66, 67, 74, 75,
  77, 83, 84, 86, 88, 90, 93, 119, 121
Guernsey Airport 23, 24, 56, 57, 83, 86,
  90, 91

Halifax, Handley Page 13, 14, 113, 133
Haverfordwest Airfield 85
Hawarden Airport 77
Herald, Handley Page 40, 63, 85, 92, 154
Hermes, Handley Page 17, 27, 30, 31, 32,
  33, 58, 96, 100, 102, 104, 107, 116, 117,
  121, 122, 125, 140, 154
Heron, De Havilland 21, 24, 36, 55, 56,
  62, 65, 68, 72, 73, 75, 76, 80, 81, 86, 90,
  91, 153
HS-125 139
Hunter, Hawker 139
Hunting-Clan Air Transport (and Hunting
  Air Travel) 23, 34, 56, 61, 67, 68, 81,
  95, 97, 99, 104, 121

Iberia 63
Icelandair 62
International Air Transport Association
  (IATA) 68, 93
Invicta Airways 125
Ipswich Airport 93
Island Air Services 93, 129
Islay Airport 63
Isle of Man 65, 67, 70, 72, 73, 74, 77, 80,
  83, 84, 105, 110, 115
Isle of Wight 68, 71, 72, 80, 82, 83, 110

Jersey Airlines 55, 56, 73, 80, 81, 89, 91,
  93, 110, 111
Jersey Airpoint 21, 23, 24, 56, 57, 67, 70,
  71, 72, 77, 80, 83, 84, 86, 90, 91, 93,
  110, 112, 118
JU52/3M, Junkers 12

KLM 33, 36, 39, 81

Laker, Freddie 14, 45, 102, 110, 136
Lancashire Aircraft Corporation 14, 70,
  72, 99, 105, 113, 132, 133
Lancastrian, Avro 9, 11, 12, 13
Land's End Airfield 23, 87, 90
Languedoc, Sud Est 33
Leeds/Bradford (Yeadon) Airport 68, 70,
  71, 72, 90
Leciester Airport 83
Leopard Moth, De Havilland 131
Liberator, Consolidated 14
Liverpool (Speke) Airport 14, 63, 74, 75,
  76, 77, 84, 85, 86, 88, 90, 112, 115, 119,
  123

Lockheed 12A 139
Loftleidir 50, 52, 62
London Airport 9, 10, 11, 12, 22, 23, 27,
  28, 29, 32, 33, 34, 35, 36, 37, 39, 40, 41,
  43, 44, 45, 46, 47, 48, 49, 50, 52, 56, 57,
  61, 62, 63, 64, 65, 66, 68, 70, 72, 75, 76,
  77, 79, 80, 81, 82, 83, 88, 89, 90, 96, 97,
  99, 103, 104, 109, 116, 117, 120, 129,
  144
Lufthansa 34, 48
Lundy Island 132
Luton Airport 73, 114, 123, 124, 131,
  135, 139
Lydd Airport 107, 110, 111, 112, 120
Lympne Airport 105, 106, 109, 110, 111

Manchester Airport 22, 34, 40, 46, 47, 48,
  50, 52, 62, 63, 64, 66, 68, 74, 77, 78, 79,
  80, 81, 82, 83, 84, 86, 88, 90, 91, 101,
  104, 119, 120, 121, 123, 124, 125
Manston Airport 104, 107, 125
Manx Airlines 72, 74
Marathon, Miles 84, 133
Mayflower Air Services 88, 89
McAlpine Aviation 139
Mercury Airlines 82, 88
Messenger, Miles 133, 135
Ministry of Aviation 21, 63
Ministry of Civil Aviation 9, 11, 70, 99,
  102, 109
Ministry of Supply 144, 146
Morton Air Services 23, 24, 56, 86
Mosquito, De Havilland 137
Murray Chown Aviation 86

Newcastle (Woolsington) Airport 23, 65,
  67, 68, 70, 72, 74, 75, 76, 77, 82, 83, 86,
  88, 90, 121, 123
Newquay Airport 23, 63, 77, 78, 82, 88,
  89, 90
Newtownards Airport 110
Northampton Airport 84, 131
Northolt Airport 11, 12, 21, 22, 23, 27,
  29, 34, 62, 64, 65, 66, 67, 68, 70, 72, 83,
  90, 109, 129, 140
North-South Airlines 72, 90
North Star, Canadair 43, 64, 120, 152
Nottingham Airport 84

Olley Air Service 23, 24, 56, 86
One-Eleven, BAC 57, 58, 65, 82, 152
Orkney 66
Overseas Aviation 56, 64, 120, 124
Oxford Airport 84

Panair Do Brasil 9
Pan American Airways 11, 27, 31, 39, 43,
  44, 45, 46, 47, 48, 49, 50, 52, 117
Pegasus Airlines 56, 73
Penzance Heliport 87
Piaggio P.166 139

Plymouth Airport   77, 86, 88, 91
Poole   17
Prentice, Percival   131, 136
Prestwick Airport   11, 21, 22, 43, 45, 46,
    47, 48, 52, 62, 64, 120, 137, 144
Princess, Saunders Roe   144, 145, 146
Proctor, Percival   12, 131, 133, 135

QANTAS   9, 10, 12, 33, 37

Ramsgate Airfield   131
Rapide, De Havilland   11, 12, 23, 36, 55,
    62, 70, 74, 75, 80, 83, 84, 85, 86, 87, 88,
    89, 90, 91, 92, 93, 105, 113, 115, 129,
    131, 132, 139, 153
Rearsby Airfield   137
Redhill Aerodrome   135
Riddle Airlines   58
Rollason Aircraft and Engines   135
Rotodyne, Fairey   146
Rylands, Eric   105

S-51, Sikorsky   12, 55, 74, 83
S-55, Sikorsky   35, 36, 83, 90
S-61, Sikorsky   87
SABENA   31, 46, 48, 50, 51, 58, 77, 80,
    82, 110
SAM   126
Sandringham, Short   18
Scillonian Air Services   90
Scilly Isles (St Mary's)   87, 88, 90
Scott, Sheila   140
Scottish Airlines   14, 22, 64, 100
Scottish Aviation   62
Shetland   64, 66
Shoreham Airport   93
Silver City Airways   14, 23, 55, 58, 65,
    72, 73, 74, 104, 105, 107, 109, 110, 111,
    112, 116, 120
Skyways Ltd   14, 61, 96, 99, 101, 102,
    105, 106, 107, 110, 114, 116, 117, 123
Skyways Coach-Air   72, 106, 107
Solent, Short   17, 18, 19, 99, 155
South African Airways   27, 30, 33, 117
Southampton (Eastleigh) Airport   80, 90,
    91, 110, 112
Southampton Water   17, 18, 19, 27
Southend Airport   14, 56, 71, 93, 102,
    109, 110, 112, 113, 119, 120, 121, 122,
    136, 139
SPANTAX   126
Stansted Airport   96, 97, 100, 101, 102,
    104, 113, 117
Starliner, Lockheed   48, 49, 50, 154
Starways   63, 75, 76, 77, 82, 88, 90, 119,
    123

Staverton Airport   84, 86, 90
Stratocruiser, Boeing   28, 39, 43, 44, 46,
    152
Sudan Airways   56
Sunderland, Short (including Hythe class)
    13, 17, 18
Super Constellation, Lockheed   33, 36, 37,
    47, 48, 49, 58, 154
Swansea Airport   24, 56, 86
Swissair   47

Teesside Airport   70, 82
Thomson, Adam   109
Thruxton Airfield   136
Thruxton Jackaroo   136, 140
Tiger Club   135
Tiger Moth, De Havilland   133, 135, 136
Tiree   62
Tradair   93, 120Transair   23, 24, 55, 56,
    103, 116, 120
Trans-Canada Air Lines   11, 43, 45, 47,
    49, 50, 52, 64, 120
Trans-European Aviation   123
Transocean Airlines   47
Trans World Airlines   43, 44, 45, 46, 47,
    48, 49, 50
Trident, De Havilland   41, 82, 153
TU-104, Tupolev   36, 39, 155
Tudor, Avro (including Supertrader)   14,
    97, 102, 113

VC-10, Vickers   41, 52, 58, 104, 155
Vanguard, Vickers   39, 63, 64, 65, 155
Viking, Vickers   11, 12, 14, 21, 22, 23, 27,
    34, 56, 62, 68, 70, 73, 76, 79, 81, 82, 90,
    93, 95, 97, 99, 102, 113, 116, 119, 120,
    121, 124, 125, 155
Viscount, Vickers   21, 27, 31, 33, 34, 36,
    39, 41, 55, 56, 57, 62, 63, 65, 66, 68, 72,
    77, 79, 80, 81, 82, 83, 84, 87, 90, 91, 93,
    97, 103, 104, 107, 119, 120, 121, 125,
    155

War Office   99, 101, 102
Western Airways   12
West Hartlepool (Greatham) Airport   67,
    68
Weston-super-Mare Airfield   12, 23, 85
White Waltham Airfield   140
William Dempster Ltd   113
Wolverhampton Airfield   83, 84, 138
Woodvale Airfield   110
Wright Aviation   75

Yeadon Aviation   70
York, Avro   10, 27, 34, 40, 81, 96, 99,
    100, 101, 102, 114, 115, 116, 117, 151